God Only Knows

"In *God Only Knows*, Herb Gruning uses a very personal and colorfully anecdotal style to make a usually dry and technical topic readable and accessible. His treatment of the features of three theistic systems of thought, and their biblical and philosophical origins, exposing both the strengths and the weaknesses of each, is entertaining and incisive. Unlike many authors he is not afraid to state his preference, nor to criticize even his own position. At times I wanted to scream in disagreement, at others I laughed at his total lack of pomposity and his irreverence toward the cherished sacred bovines of philosophy and religion. I would like to see what he might do with the less traditionally theistic systems that many find more convincing today."

—**Rev. David Reid**

"In this uniquely organized book Herb Gruning tackles intriguing issues of metaphysical import in the interface between science and religion. Questions broached include God's nature and God's relationship to a world known through the marvels of modern science. Gruning rather roguishly samples extant positions keen to settle matters by appealing to religious or scientific magisteria. There's something here for everyone. Believers will appreciate the solicitous treatment of cherished beliefs while specialists (perhaps believers themselves), anesthetized by the jejune rhetoric of scientific materialists and biblical literalists, will welcome the balanced treatment of differing views. Gruning steers a middle course between classical theism and panentheism. In fact, he comes out just left of the 'openness' model, a newcomer to the debate, which mitigates the concerns of both theisms. Whether the case he makes is true, of course, God only knows."

—**Jim Kanaris**, Ph.D., Faculty Lecturer
in Philosophy of Religion, McGill University

"I see a wild opportunity for potential new audiences with this book. As I read, I've been sharing ideas from it with my more sarcastic, skeptical, and scientific friends. Their reactions have been wonderful. When a career-pessimist laughs with surprise at hearing a new concept of divinity or man's relation to God that he thinks is clever brand new, then you know you have a winner. I hope that this book will find its way into the hands of exactly that kind of person. I think that Dr. Gruning is giving us an opportunity to think in new ways about biology and God, but also just to think in new ways.

"This book has personality, is quick to read, and is also very important. We're living in a decade when science and religion are supposedly at odds. We need to be focused on the serious moral issues of our time, but this other popular debate about Darwin and Christ is dividing us. This book is indispensable because those of us who are familiar with evolution and genetics also need to discover the variations of divinity that are being talked about with regard to science. Herb Gruning teaches us the vocabulary that will help the atheist or the agnostic to get along with those who keep the faith, with respect and understanding for spiritual matters in the 21st century.

"Funny, readable, short and sweet, this book starts conversations. Each section has ways of getting people excited about concepts from science and divinity that they haven't thought of before. Christians can appreciate the way that Herb Gruning renews their options for living with faith while accepting science. Meanwhile, even the most dedicated cynic can find enjoyment in these new ways of thinking about God and the world."

—**Terry Trowbridge**, M.A. candidate in Social Justice
and Equity Studies, Brock University, Canada

"Gruning possesses an amazing ability to render complex subjects in clear concise prose that would normally require several tomes of dense explanation. Witty observations and unexpected alliterations abound alongside illuminating aphorisms, making this book an enjoyable read on several levels. Gruning takes you through many prevailing theological and scientific ideas, and reveals their interactions and limitations, with a generous and non-dogmatic spirit."

—**Paul van Arragon**, Ph.D.

"This is a book for people who enjoy ideas. Big ones, like the nature of God, Man, the Universe and how they all interact. Written in a playful manner, the first two-thirds of the book are spent warming up with many mental tidbits and facts from diverse fields of study. A tighter focus and heavier cerebral lifting occur in the more serious final third. Every human must have some answers for these big questions, and like a well-stocked kitchen or gymnasium, this book has something for everyone to work with. The thinking and the thoughts are serious and deep, but the manner is light because the author has humility about his field of study. Theologians must know they can never completely define God, and therefore *God Only Knows* the accuracy of our thoughts."

—**David Rempel**, D.D.S.

"Dr. Gruning's book stands as an essential introduction, for students and educated laypeople, in the area of how to think about God in light of our modern understanding of the world. How does God fit in with science? Does science tell us anything about God? Examining the works of theologians, philosophers and scientists such as David Ray Griffin, Charles Hartshorne, John Polkinghorne and Lyall Watson, Dr. Gruning gives a clear and accessible account of what science and theology today can tell us about the God-world relation. In my forty-four years as an industrial worker, with an interest in amateur astronomy, this book could have done much to help clarify my confusion over the apparent rift between the science that I found so compelling, and the religion that called from my heart. This is a fitting companion to Gruning's previous book *God and the New Metaphysics*."

—**Keith Sudds**, retired industrial worker
and amateur astronomer

God Only Knows

Piecing Together
the Divine Puzzle

HERB GRUNING

BLUE DOLPHIN PUBLISHING

Published by Blue Dolphin Publishing, Inc.
P.O. Box 8, Nevada City, CA 95959
Orders: 1-800-643-0765
Web: www.bluedolphinpublishing.com

ISBN: 978-1-57733-240-4

Library of Congress Cataloging-in-Publication Data

Gruning, Herb.
    God only knows : piecing together the divine puzzle / Herb Gruning.
        p. cm.
    Includes bibliographical references.
    ISBN 978-1-57733-240-4 (pbk. : alk. paper)
    1. God. 2. Open theism. I. Title.
    BL473.G78 2009
    211'.3--dc22

                                                    2009021827

Printed in the United States of America

10   9   8   7   6   5   4   3   2   1

Dedication

For Alice

Contents

Foreword

A GIFFORD LECTURER recently spoke of the surprising return of God in very recent times. Well, at least there has been—interestingly enough since 9/11!—a surprising return of interest in the God question, even if expressed in the form of attacks on theistic belief. But the quality of the attacks has been uneven, with much of it consisting of semi-popular publications, containing more aggressive assertions than careful argument. And this has provoked a good number of defensive replies in kind from believers. But there are, happily, some whose medium of thinking and communicating is calm, steady, insightful, and who exhibit self-critical reflectiveness. Herb Gruning's *God Only Knows* is a first-rate representative of this approach.

Gruning is a convinced believer, though not dogmatic or defensive. His writing contains no heated rhetoric, no rousing appeals to deep prejudices, fears, or resentments, no razzle-dazzle, no scoundrels to be scalped and disemboweled, no shotgun blasts of names directed at the reader or a fog of jargon; there is just a sincere invitation to fellow seekers to join him in thinking clearly and insightfully with the best available science, philosophy, theology, and religious studies.

Gruning's style is in the spirit of classical learning and philosophy—but he hardly takes refuge in traditional positions. For example, while he is appreciative of certain biblical themes and motifs, he is far from being dismissive of Enlightenment objections and newer/higher criticisms. But he seeks out the heavenly treasure while discarding flawed and outdated earthen vessels, what someone has called "period trash" from another age.

One of the ways of distinguishing treasure from outmoded vessels is, for Gruning, the test of modern understandings of nature and the history of science. Hence throughout his book he shows the benefit of a well-informed and thought-provoking discussion of the physical world, and includes his own surprising discoveries of places where the natural seems to open out into what he does not hesitate to call supernatural!

Belief in God must, Gruning holds, not only be constrained by what we learn from science, it must also do justice to abiding religious sensibilities. And a central one is the intimation of divine perfection. But while everyone who believes in God at all believes that God is perfection, very significant differences come into play as to what constitutes perfection (and this matters, given the injunction that we should seek to emulate the perfection of God).

Gruning identifies a variety of major options—including classical or traditional theism, panentheism, and so-called "openness theism." While traditional theism, rooted in Greek philosophy, thinks of perfection in terms of independence rather than relatedness, being rather than becoming, power rather than persuasion, the other two options reverse the valuation of these polar opposites. They find in this major revision a way of thinking that is not only more religiously appropriate but also more philosophically adequate. However, while panentheism is rather well-known and well-developed, openness theism, so-named anyway, is a fresh arrival on the scene, and there are differences as well as similarities between the two that promise to be interesting. But they are also in need of sorting out. Gruning has contributed to this task in his book and suggests guidelines where further work can and should be done.

Finally, there is Gruning's proposal that the aesthetic is worthy of being granted equality vis à vis moral goodness in thinking about perfection. Adopting this could enrich our understanding of both divine providence and human virtue. Gruning says just enough to tantalize us and to give us direction for future thought.

Gruning's is a well-furnished and insightful mind. I'm glad he is among those engaged in the rethinking of the question of God.

Dr. John C. Robertson
Professor Emeritus, Department of Religious Studies
McMaster University, Hamilton, Ontario, Canada

Acknowledgments

I WISH TO THANK
all those who reviewed this volume
prior to its publication

Introducing

I LIKE BOOKS. Lots of them. The more the merrier. For me, less is not more; more is an improvement. Yet to the extent that I am able to satisfy my paper predilections, it is also incumbent upon me to impose order on my environment in the interest of space. (When asked to defend the virtues of books against those who are unconvinced and value space at a premium, in desperation I play the card of promoting books as affording some degree of insulation and soundproofing.) And when this need cannot be met through handyman efforts or local used and discount furniture outlets, given my penchant for fiscal responsibility, I reluctantly turn to new shelves from locations which have a distinctly Scandinavian flavor.

Should these items be secured from the latter establishment, and through the assistance of neighbors whose vehicles bear sufficient carrying capacity, the boxes are opened and the contents are spilled out onto the floor. Now not only the boxes but also the means to house the books are in disarray. All that stands in the way of orderliness then are a screwdriver—a makeshift one often included in the package—elbow grease (which is not) and the instructions. Hopefully before long, and a suitable amount of kinetic energy, books are organized on shelves and floor space is restored, whereupon I am reminded by a grateful spouse that this is what the carpet looks like.

Perhaps a similar situation occurred with the divinity. Imagine the excitement of having a bunch of new things around, awaiting them to conform to order. But then where in the world would you put them? Hey that's it—a world! One difference, and at the same time an advantage, for the deity, at least the traditional one, is that there is ultimately not the same constraints on space. No need to consult anything Scandinavian.

It is precisely this traditional view that I wish to explore. When considering how the creation got underway, the debate usually centers on, as David Ray Griffin informs us, the two sides of creation out of nothing (creatio ex nihilo) and creation out of chaos. In the case of the former, there was no preexistent matter that did not have a divine origin. Since the entire length and breadth of universal matter had the deity as its source, in this view God also has a claim on it and power over it. Its power, to the extent that it enjoys any, is delegated power and this can be withdrawn or overridden at any time. The amount of power that God relinquishes is exactly the amount that the creatures can command, and the two together equal one hundred percent. Since the creation boasts no native power of its own, omnipotence (meaning all-powerful) can be retained as a theological category, in this case an attribute of God, in the traditional sense. The only power God does not have is that which God gives away.

In the case of the latter, there was preexistent matter known as chaos out of which the divinity formed a world of order. Power in this case is shared. Chaotic matter already has inherent power, meaning God does not have a monopoly on it. The mindset of the followers of Alfred North Whitehead, referred to as process thinkers, Griffin being one of the main exponents, favor this scenario since in the place of an authoritarian, coercive deity comes a persuasive one—one which is hands-on with respect to vested interests and coaxing creatures toward these ends, but hands-off in terms of effectual, unilateral activity.

The present book has three aims and comes in three parts. It first seeks to interact with the traditional Judeo-Christian scriptures to determine what sense can be made of them for life in the twenty-first century and to what extent they are still worth investing in. An overarching question put to them will be whether or not the God depicted therein is a misrepresentation of the one which actually manifests itself. In some cases, we will be asking how God is related to the natural world, implying that our commentary on the biblical text will often have a scientific import. The second aim is to investigate this natural world that is so often highlighted in these same scriptures. To this end we will examine the work of biologist Lyall Watson. The final section will analyze three models of divinity with the foregoing in mind. These inquiries and reflections will yield three questions: what kind of divinity might there be?; what kind of world are we working with?; and what kind of relation would these two likely have? The inspiration for several of the lines of inquiry pursued here stems from the work entitled *The Paradox of God and the Science of Omniscience* by Clifford A. Pickover. While the current volume is not in direct response to Pickover's arguments, it does take them into account.

Topics covered in the biblical segment will generally follow the order in which they are treated in the Judeo-Christian scriptures themselves. Themes in the science component will then take their cues from the writings of Watson. Images of God will round out the third. It appears that the best place to start would be at the beginning, with a more theological discussion about an alleged creation. Upon completion of my set purposes in this threefold study, God only knows where the discussion ultimately will lead.

PART ONE

Message in a Bible

Creating

*Genesis 1:1-2—In the beginning when God created the heavens and
the earth, the earth was formless and void and darkness covered the face
of the deep, while a wind from God swept over the face of the waters.
(All biblical references are drawn from the NRSV—the New Revised
Standard Version—unless otherwise noted.)*

THE QUESTION I WISH TO RAISE is whether or not there can be a two-
step approach to creation. Is it likely that God, in what amounts
to a first stage of creation, could have created all the parts, all the
raw materials necessary for subsequent construction plans? At
this point, God could have exclaimed, "What a mess! But all is
ready." Together with this chaos, God could have conferred on it
a creative potential of its own which was about to be set in mo-
tion. As a parent sends a child off to college, the parent allows the
offspring to grow toward intellectual and moral maturity, knowing full well that numerous mistakes will be made along the way.
So too could God have opened the door to enabling the chaos to
become a cosmos, the parting words constituting instructions or
directions on the best way to get there. This would be analogous
to the above parent who hopes the child will benefit from the parent's wisdom and its own experiences. Lastly, the parent extends
wishes of farewell and a reminder that s/he will always be only a
holler away.

A divinity who operates like a parent, to the extent that such
a model is successful, would engage in a voluntary self-limitation

on power, with the creation enjoying genuine self-determination. Yet what is given could also be taken away, making this characterization different from a deistic approach in which the deity no longer assumes an active role in the creation once it is underway. This God would be active once, at the outset, and thereafter is entirely withdrawn from the scene. But God as a parent would divest God's self of the need to intervene every time there is a perceived concern—a temptation to step in. This promotes the assurance on the part of the child that it enjoys the latitude to find its own way on the path to personal development, come what may. As a parent proudly rejoices over the successes of its offspring, so too would it agonize over its failures. These are the risks involved in parenthood.

With the aforementioned in mind, some commentators might object that a parental deity simply places God at one remove from the traditional/classical divinity that we have grown accustomed to (and perhaps also tired of). My response is that this might be the step that is required to address the vexing question of God's power and goodness in relation to the persistent instances of evil in the world. The additional stage mentioned above could provide a missing puzzle piece that may, at least in part, overcome some of the difficulties. Recalling a theme from the introduction, as a disorder of books and shelf components are organized into a library, so might God have spread the parts out on the "floor" or workbench area before beginning to establish some semblance of order, leaving them in some, or perhaps many, cases to receive assistance upon request. While not completely successful, the analogy is partially helpful in seeing how creaturely initiative can fit with divine goodness and power. Unlike the process divinity, who can only ever operate persuasively, this God does not fail to nudge at certain points. That especially heinous crimes and egregious evils are perpetrated by humans means that parents are limited in their authority, albeit in this God's case it is self-imposed.

What has been outlined briefly here has in recent history been described as indicative of a third approach to divinity referred to as the openness model, spearheaded by Clark Pinnock and others. It lies somewhere in between the two extremes of the classical and process deities, as a third alternative. But this is to anticipate Part Three. (I request the reader to indulge me in this foretaste of topics to follow.) Now that the creation has been established in our account, what remains is to determine which approach can best deal with its counterpart, namely evolution. Perhaps we still need more than the ordinary workings of the process God to drive such a mechanism. The "traditional God" has all the power and determines all things, although softer approaches to the classical view can also be taken. The "process God" has diminished power and can, with qualification, determine nothing. The "openness God" had all the power, retains most of it, and determines some things. Which fits in best with standard evolutionary doctrine?

To begin with, it does not take much to alter the structure of genetic material—break a hydrogen bond here and form another one there and the result is a different nucleic acid, which can, in turn, lead to a different evolutionary history. The trouble is that this strategy, despite not needing much energetic input, still requires something. Breaking and forming are not activities of which the Whiteheadian divinity is considered capable, unless there is a greater capacity to the function of persuasion or luring than is customarily understood. Activities such as these are typical of the language employed when referring to a more interventionist deity who temporarily suspends the regularities of the world so as to effect a change that would not ordinarily result if left to itself. Would a divinity that operates solely on the basis of lure be able to effect the kind of changes that are expected in the evolutionary theater? If breaking and forming are terms which one insists must be included in the evolutionary scheme, then this sounds too coercive for a process deity.

What must necessarily be upheld in the Whiteheadian system is the self-determinative power of entities. God is never in a position to override what creatures will do with their freedom. This makes freedom authentic and genuine, if not extensive. God is still regarded as the most irresistible force in the universe; yet this must remain a force that can be resisted by those entities boasting the wherewithal to do so—normally taken to be those possessing consciousness. Those that do not are relegated mostly to repeating the past, from which we obtain our notion of physical laws. Self-determination cannot be violated and both the world and God evolve in such an undertaking.

In the course of this development, natural laws, too, can become modified. But this is different from taking liberties with them. In the traditional approach, natural laws prevail upon entities. These laws tend to be understood in a Platonic sense, where they exist independently of the particles that must conform to them. Yet it is sometimes forgotten that these laws are descriptions, approximate in their precision, of the behavior of objects. No particles (or fields), no laws. This makes the laws universal, for there is nowhere, it is believed, that there are either no particles or fields. There are no initial laws which then act on particles. For Whitehead, there is regularity on the part of entities that cannot exercise sufficient self-determining power. To the extent that they repeat the past, in the epoch or era in which they do so, we can be relatively confident that they will abide by this regularity. This allows us to speak of order. And this order can be expressed in terms which science can quantify.

Well and good. Nevertheless, a deity that goes beyond luring and actually steers a course is not consistent with the God of Whitehead. Can the process God be relied upon then to advance the evolutionary cause? The answer on the part of process thinkers to this question is yes, though a qualified one. Using process language, that evolution has advanced must be attributed to the amenability of entities to conform to the divine lure, even though this is not guaranteed. In order to produce novelty, which is well within their ability, given God's initial input, entities must have something to work with. Such raw material is taken by evolutionary doctrine to constitute variations brought about by mutations. Can all genetic mutations, though, be accounted for through conventional means? If not, then genetic material requires a push, and a push is what the process deity cannot provide. The question remains as to whether the process God assumes the role of a true evolutionary agent. Some are led to suspect that this is not what the Whiteheadian divinity can accomplish. Anything more than this, however, crosses the line into interventionist territory, whether classical or openness. Are we led to believe that we are left with no other alternative? The prospect is that we may have to live with this and remain at an impasse. Once again, we will address these themes more fully in Part Three, a preview of which has been given here. But now back to the biblical accounts.

Verses 26-27: Then God said,"Let us make humankind in our image, according to our likeness;...

Any creature descended from hominids is human. So we were not the only human species. We are just the last surviving ones. Humans are described in the verses above as being created in the image of God. If that extends to all humans, then consequently all species of humans are naturally human. This implies that, for example, the Neanderthals were human. They might very well have been the first ones to bury their dead, thereby recognizing the significance of birth and death—the beginning and ending of life—our mortality. And they apparently accorded it some meaning in their rituals. Perhaps they too wrestled with existentialist themes. Religiosity or spirituality, or at least metaphysical speculation, therefore, may not have originated with us. Our species, if different from the Neanderthals (a theory which goes in and out of fashion), would then need to settle for second place in the race for God-consciousness.

Yet if all human species are created in God's image and we are the only members left to engage in theological discourse about it, then it would seem that neither natural selection nor God place too much stock in our own perceived elevated status. The image does not guarantee longevity. And whether or not this makes a species more valuable, the least we can say is that to be an image-bearer does not automatically grant us a place in God's protective custody. We are left to fend with natural selection as best we can, and only one of our species ultimately could. Other image-bearers were considered expendable.

Moreover, our survival might have come at the expense of other human species. If there were insufficient resources for multiple human species to flourish, then we won out over our Neanderthal cousins. We appear to have a history of victories in the struggle for existence. Long live the competitive spirit, I suppose.

If confronted with this issue, some theists might inject a moral component into the proceedings and suggest that only one human species demonstrated itself as worthy of survival—a strategy of reading into natural selection more than is warranted scientifically. For in Christian terms, to be in God's favor is not something that we can merit. To think that we survived because we were worth the attention is the height of hubris. Others might object that to find oneself in a certain human lineage does not guarantee the same essential status. Maybe *Homo sapiens* are the only species to have been blessed with the divine image, meaning the biblical text requires modification based on more current anthropological findings. Like with Abraham in the Hebrew tradition, the choice of which species gets the image is as arbitrary on God's part as who gets to be chosen as the father of many nations. If so, then human observances like burial rituals were not enough to elevate the status of non-image-bearing creatures. Was God running God's own experiment as to which species would prove themselves as suitable templates for the image? In any case, now only one species gets to solemnize a burial. Sorry for the inconvenience.

The Calling

> Genesis 2:15—*The LORD God took the man and put him in the garden of Eden to till it and keep it.*

Whereas Genesis 1 discusses the origin of the universe and our planet within it, Genesis 2 addresses the origin of humans. What makes humans different from other species? There are certain animals, like racoons, that have been known to wash their food prior to ingesting it. In this way they are like us in our more hygienic moments. Yet there may be no other species that, at least in the main of civility, cleans up after itself. In the animal world, predators leave the remains of prey for scavengers to finish off, and what scavengers do not claim is left to decomposers. What is worse, other animals evacuate their colons and bladders, should they come equipped with them, wherever and whenever their physiology prompts. Humans, at least those with the presence of mind and accompanying forethought, observe cultural norms of sanitation as often as possible.

This is reminiscent of Genesis 2:15 where, in this mythological genre of literature, humans are called upon to tend and take care of the then known world. We are given the mandate to be custodians of the planet, for no one else will, or has been given the job. It seems the task has been delegated to us. Perhaps even more precisely, since the Genesis myth has the first humans in a garden, we might better be described as gardeners. But even gardeners are custodians of a certain sort. Each spring, those who fancy themselves as plant health professionals, as well as others less qualified, perform the unenviable chore of "weedectomy." Gardeners must clean the area and prepare the soil before introducing new inhabitants or enticing current ones to thrive. No species other than humans are agriculturalists and much of what they do amounts to cultural activities. Other species form collectives, such as the social insects like ants, bees, termites and wasps. Yet it would be a stretch to construe their engagements as the makings of a culture as such, even though similar language can be employed. Species can display habits and instinct, but only humans appeal to tradition. Bees perform dances—movements geared toward communicating the whereabouts of the most tantalizing nectar—while humans perform rites. Elephants return to graveyards; humans bring flowers, wreaths, and erect stones and crosses.

It appears that God was interested in having somebody take on the daily duties attending to an agricultural region while enjoying life within it. For this God needed gardener-custodians. (The portrait in Genesis 1 differs in several respects from that of Genesis 2, where humans were created earlier on.) Whereas in Mark's account (2:27), the gospel writer has Jesus declare that humans were not made for the Sabbath but the Sabbath for humans, the reverse is the case here in the Genesis tale: the creation seems not to have been made for humans but humans for the creation. Some might argue that humans are what the creation was leading up to; but a case could also be made that humans were an afterthought—with God motioning to God's heavenly court that now that there is a creation, one supposes we should have someone look after it. Better consult the yellow pages under caretakers or domestics.

The Undoing

> Genesis 3:14, 17-19—*The LORD God said to the serpent, "...cursed are you among all animals/ and among all wild creatures;/ upon your belly you shall go,/ and dust you shall eat/ all the days of your life..." And to the man he said, "...cursed is the ground because of you;/ in toil you shall eat of it all the days of your life;/ thorns and thistles it shall bring forth for you;/...By the sweat of your face you shall eat bread..."*

One can well imagine what might have prompted the author(s) to write the accounts of the first chapters of Genesis as they did. It does not require a keen observer to recognize that successes for some creatures are matched or offset by failures for others. Not only does sweat become a concomitant for earning a living (Gen. 3:17-19), but some organisms are sentenced to a horizontal livelihood, while others more vertical (Gen. 3:14). The notion that "nature is red in tooth and claw" must also have struck the ancients and not first been evident to nineteenth-century Englishmen like Lord Tennyson. The capture and conquest of the unfortunate organisms enables others to survive. Even if they were not inclined to think in those terms, this type of occurrence must have appeared as a universal rule of thumb or law of nature to all who cared to look, in any era. No creature, humans included, are exempt from some type of toilsome labor for purposes of sustenance, and this will have an impact upon the wider environment.

What may not have been so immediately apparent, though, is the conviction that things were not always this way. Through the efforts of an active imagination, some humans were driven to conclude that the current state of affairs is the way things *became*, not how they originated or were initially intended. Only in part, would some have contended, do they now reflect the primordial craftsmanship. For the ancient Hebrews, things were understood to have been fine for a while and then they went wrong. Due to a human misadventure, the higher powers were disposed to place these primeval humans into a setting in which they would need to fend for themselves. In theological terms this is known as the Fall. Perhaps the story is analogous to an adolescent who gets kicked out of the house for failure to be a team (family) member or player. The difference is that, in the religious sphere, the debarment is permanent, and the effect could be felt on a global scale. This amounts to an erstwhile explanation as to why the experienced world behaves as it does; an account about which only millennia later would we learn to refer to in Malthusian-Darwinian terms. The earth is a messy place, but was it always this way? Perhaps the ancients were dealing with a similar question and gave it a pre-biological dress.

At times the Bible is ambiguous on certain fronts. More than one theological tradition is able to find support for its views therein. The debates surrounding the doctrinal issues of predestination, election (is salvation our choice or God's?) and perseverance (can one lose or fall away from the faith after one obtains it?) are equally corroborated from the scriptures. If one were to ask what the biblical view is on these topics, the answer would be that there are multiple defensible ones. But which one is right? Can more than one be right? Perhaps this calls for wisdom to unlock the mystery of this sacred text. We will return to these questions in Part Three.

There is another mystery, or wisdom, that might be embedded in the text. In the mythical account of the first human pair having eaten of the forbidden fruit from the tree of the knowledge of good and evil, there may lie a truth about anthropological evolutionary history. When our primogenitors first rose to consciousness, a number of changes would have occurred. The Genesis text speaks of the eyes of both Adam and Eve being opened such that they recognized that they were naked. This appears not to be a concern for any other species. (Nor seemingly is it problematic for nudist beaches and colonies, but at least the participants understand the import and legal/social ramifications, else they would not go to these lengths.) Consciousness then seems to bring with it some kind of barometer or moral compass, gauging appropriate behavior. When it first struck humans that nakedness could bring with it shame, a recourse was devised, meaning both plants and animals have borne the brunt of our pursuit of modesty. We have killed to clothe.

What triggered the response was no doubt emotive. Consciousness and conscience evidently generated the concepts of "should" and "ought." The creatures that bore it felt a need to take stock of heretofore standard operating procedures. To continue on the same course would be to become subject to a new feeling, which would put the individual ill at ease. These feelings and how to alleviate them developed into social norms, customs and notions of acceptability, which then called for a modification of behavior so as to ensure communal cohesion. Perhaps this new found capability of consciousness came to be looked upon as more trouble than it was worth. Yet we are stuck with it. It comes with the territory.

According to the mythical accounts, when first confronted with the shamefulness of what was up to then acceptable behavior, the first conscious human pair sought to cover their nakedness initially with fig leaves (Genesis 3:7) and later the God of the text provided them with "garments of skin" in order to clothe them (Genesis 3:21). When God charged them with disobedience, their reflex reaction was to pass the buck of responsibility. Adopting a defensive posture became a way to deflect personal emotive injury inflicted on oneself or others. When one's character is called into question, the response is often to point the finger elsewhere. Perhaps humans were never built to carry the burden of guilt. Hospitals and courts of law can attest to the harm that follows the attempted deflection of culpability. Along with the naming of all the animals (Genesis 2:19-20), humans would eventually compile a list of terms, a vocabulary, to describe the conditions associated with the inability to come to grips with feelings and our responses to them, such as repression, denial, illusion, dysfunction, neurotic and psychotic. Naming things gives us some measure of power and control. Maybe then we can cope. But at least we have the knowledge of good and evil. No one, not even God, can take that away from us. That's a plus, right?

(The following is inspired by chapter 8 of the Pickover volume indicated above.)

There are certain enigmas which persist about the first chapters of Genesis. Despite the mythical nature of the accounts, taking them at face value for the sake of argument can reward another theological look. For instance, there is a longstanding debate about the reasonableness, even the justifiability, of God's dealings with Eve concerning the forbidden fruit. The difficulty surrounds her knowledge of the morality of the situation, which can be outlined this way: 1) It is right to obey God; 2) God commands not to eat of the fruit; 3) It would be wrong to break this command. Some authors, like Pickover and those whom he cites, then appear to make the move of having Eve undertake an ethical evaluation of the position in which she finds herself. They seem to substitute the term "good" for "right" in statement 1) above and "evil" for "wrong" in 3). They conclude thereby that she already had knowledge of good and evil prior to eating the fruit, with which she was able to assess the moral consequences for herself. If she did not, nothing could be held against her for eating, they argue. If she did, then there would be no reason to eat the fruit for purposes of securing a faculty which she already possessed. Nor would it then have held any attraction for her so that she might be tempted.

One way out of this conundrum is to claim that there occurs in the above argumentation an equivocation of the term "know(ledge)." I find that the use of the word in Pickover's example is too broad; a distinction needs to be made between the two types, namely, Eve had knowledge of good and evil, but she did not have knowledge of it. In the first instance, she had the type of knowledge that amounts to an awareness of a directive and an expectation as well as a dire warning of consequences. In the second, she did not have an intimate experience of good and evil prior to eating. Since there are consequences only for a violation of the second, once the first is in place, the God of the text is therefore justified in punishing Eve for her misdeeds. Maybe this suffices.

But the fun does not stop there, for there were two trees of note in the Garden. The tree of the knowledge of good and evil was in the middle of the Garden, yet also in the same spot was the tree of life. Both Adam and Eve had access to this as well as permission to eat from it. God provided the pair with ample food to eat, though was it the tree of life which kept them from perishing? Apparently, death was a possibility, even in Eden. In either case, there was an additional way to die, as portrayed earlier. The text is not clear, however, as to what precisely is the cause of this "surely dying." Is it the function or result of physically eating the fruit, or morally transgressing God's injunction, or cognitively knowing good and evil, or being subjected to God's curse? What is more, the "surely dying" of Genesis 2:17 is not so certain, since 3:22 stipulates that the pair must be prevented from access to the tree of life for they would otherwise live forever. There is thus another element to add to the calculations: fallen, corrupted humans can still enjoy a never-ending existence unless they are denied access to this tree. To make matters even more complex, what would the concept of death have meant to them if they had not as yet been faced with any? Presumably death had not entered the world, but at least the pair would have been clear as to what constitutes disobedience to God. But not so with death. Then why threaten them with death if the term was without content for them?

Back on the subject of the tree of life—did its fruit need to be eaten regularly or only once? And for that matter, how did they dispose of waste products? As for a related instance that is somewhat less legendary, if only for being committed to writing much closer to the alleged event and more recent to our time (as opposed to accounts written not even remotely close to their proposed occurrences, such as the Genesis creation story), is the one of the resurrected Jesus. The same question can be applied here. The risen Jesus could seemingly be touched (Luke 24:36-43), so the resurrected body is physical in some sense and can take food. The risen Jesus presumably did not require food, so was this simply a revelatory demonstration of what such a body can do? Further, how would a risen body eliminate waste? Does the afterlife involve sanitation? There also appears the necessity to distinguish between resuscitated and resurrected bodies, for the Jesus of the text raised Lazarus from the dead, but the latter did not thereby come equipped with a resurrected frame. This implies that Lazarus bore the unenviable task of dying twice.

We are informed in the final two chapters of the last book of the Bible of a scene resplendent in beauty where the river of the water of life will flow from the throne of God and of the Lamb, and that there will be a tree of life on each side of this river, yielding a monthly harvest. There will no longer be any death in the New Jerusalem and the Genesis curse will be lifted. Though even here it looks like there will still be a need to eat regularly, otherwise why mention a continual crop? Unless the two trees need supply a vast throng only once. Supply and demand—a consideration even in the hereafter.

Judging and Liberating

Exodus 7:3-5—But I will harden Pharaoh's heart,...I will lay my hand upon Egypt...by great acts of judgment.

Exodus 14:5-9—the minds of Pharaoh and his officials were changed toward the people,...The Egyptians pursued them.

Does God set up certain people to fail? According to these passages, the divine is interested in leading the Israelites out of bondage to Pharaoh in Egypt through the display of God's mighty hand and outstretched arm. Well, if this is the case, then why wait for Pharaoh's heart to be hardened? And for that matter, why go to these lengths in the first place? There seems to be a three-step approach on God's part, two of which might be extraneous: harden Pharaoh's heart; display mighty acts of judgment in direct response to it; and bring God's people out of Egypt. Was the God of the text looking for justification in the eyes of the Egyptians for carrying out the third stage? Would skipping right ahead to step three have been interpreted by the Egyptians as an ungrateful reaction on the part of long-time boarders?, a type of eat and run, or in their case, farm and flee? Did the Egyptians first need to be impacted by the severity of the plagues so that God's work might make a lasting impression and they would then welcome the Israelites' departure? Admittedly, this effort would have more of an effect, but then the main objective would be more than the stated one of release of the slaves.

Perhaps God could not have made a name for Godself without such intervention. Otherwise the events might have been understood as Pharaoh simply having a case of weak knees in acceding to the request of the slaves. By adopting God's strategy, however, Pharaoh gets to save political face, though at the expense of the devastation of the land and the deaths of all firstborn. Imagine how much worse it would have been had Pharaoh lost the respect of his subjects—could that have been regained in short order? Yet with these methods, God gains respect (and fear and awe) and Pharaoh retains it, for a while anyway. Until such time, that is, as he changes his mind about the Israelites (although it is not clear how the author of this book was privy to Pharaoh's private conversation with his staff) and pursues them with his army. Concerning the rest, Cecil B. DeMille has provided for us a backdrop.

As for vessels used for noble or ignoble purposes, Pharaoh is an example of the latter. He, like Judas, was an instrument for destruction (and, it could be argued by traditionalists, though it might not strike them as such initially, so was Jesus). They were employed for purposes which involved their undoing. This also extends to other species. God brings a plague of locusts upon Egypt, but when God is done with them, they are given the "heave ho" into the Red Sea (Exodus 10:19). Creatures, among them certain humans, evidently, are expendable.

I do recognize that we need to guard against the tendency to discount those scriptural passages in our disfavor as failing to be indicative of the God that they describe (though perhaps this exercise for some people is putting into words what they have been thinking for some time). For maybe this is what God is like after all. Yet in Part Three we will discuss three models of divinity so as to determine which version of God best fits with the biblical data (assuming this is desirable).

Behaving

There is wisdom to be seen in the Ten Commandments (Exodus 20), and indeed the ethical monotheism of the ancient Hebrews was their genius and a great contribution to the world. Yet there appears to be a discrepancy between the injunctions and the God of the text. Particularly in the sixth commandment, the people are informed that they are not to kill. On the one hand, humans are to avoid the taking of another human life; and on the other, God can requisition it. For in closely related breaths, God tells the people not to kill, since that is wrong and ungodly, and then commands them to wipe out the nations and so reestablish their homeland. The total and utter destruction of the inhabitants of Canaan was commissioned by God and the carrying out of those orders was met with divine approval. What is disallowed for humans appears to be acceptable for the divine.

Was there anyone, I wonder, of the children of Israel who hesitated about going into Canaan and engaging in genocidal campaigns and announced, "Hey, I thought you said this was bad?" Nor is it sufficient to claim that the sacred writings at the time were liberal and liberating even for the foreigner/alien living among them, which admittedly it was, for a distinction was to be made between Israel and the nations, us and them. It was not always the case that the same rules which apply to the native-born also applied to others (Exodus 8:23; 9:4; 11:7, etc.; Deuteronomy 14:21; 15:3, etc.). The standard response on the part of those who object to this line of thinking is that the term "kill" is better interpreted as "murder," thereby making the thrust of the commandment geared more toward the proper attitude of the human heart. The message is that committing murder under your own initiative is wrong unless God sanctions it. Hence we are not to harbor such resentment toward another so that we wish ill upon him or her, so the argument runs.

Alternately, the reason for God's decision is that the inhabitants of Canaan had become idolatrous and thus had polluted the land with their idols. Destroying them can then be considered just punishment for their infractions, and God is simply using one nation to exact retribution on others. Yet the question remains: Did the Israelites ever grapple with the tension and agonize how the two injunctions are to be reconciled? Even if it were to be the case that a resolution can be found, the divinity appears to be above its own law. What is good for humans does not always apply to the God of the text. This places the law in an odd position and yields the oft-asked philosophical question: "Does God give something because it is good, or is it good because God gives it?" What is it that makes the divine moral code worthy of adherence—itself or God?

There is a further problem. The first section of the Ten Commandments refers to the fate of subsequent generations who might not have directly transgressed the same law as their predecessors or been party to their acts. There is a counter-movement in other Hebrew scriptures toward making individuals responsible for their misdeeds, not their offspring (as in Ezekiel 18, although this sentiment is also seen in writings such as Deuteronomy 24:16). Policies appeared to become modified with time. Does this mean that God had a change of heart or that humans had graduated to the point where they would adopt a different strategy? This of course assumes that the latter stage is also a more refined one and that it marks the course of progress and advancement. Or was an alternate stance chosen due to a lack of military strength where previous postures could not so easily be assumed? The language of war was not employed to nearly the same extent between the Babylonian captivity (sixth century BCE) and the Maccabean revolt (second century BCE). Did this spark a new perspective on internal and external relations? Does greater artillery might make one more or less tolerant?

Whatever the case may be, were humans the only ones who changed, while the divine simply waited like an expectant parent for the children to grow into adulthood? And were we to know the best course of action in a given situation, would we exemplify it? In any event, our view of the ancient moral code should not be from a position of ethical superiority. Before our ethical sensibilities get the better of us and so as to prevent us from undue self-righteousness, consider the following. If we are honest, we have not exactly approached our own neighbors with the height of moral rectitude. Some of those who consider it shameful the way the inhabitants of Canaan were treated by the invading Israelites (not thereby granting that these events are historically accurate) are also those whose ancestors subjugated or even drove out aboriginal peoples in North America and Australia, particularly Tasmania. For the sake of elbow room and unimpeded self-determination, we continue to exacerbate more than relieve the misery of the downtrodden. Far from objecting to the divine mandate to conquer and oust native peoples, we appear to be in the same tradition. After all, we have it in writing.

Allow me to tackle this same topic in a different way.

In the Australian Outback an Aborigine paints his body white with clay and takes part in a collective dance ritual expressing the community's connection with the earth. Over the course of some fifty thousand years they have learned a few things about the land and the role they should play in the ongoing task of marking an optimum balance between their own needs and those of the planet, at least their corner of it. A sensitivity to these needs is part of their cultural wisdom that gets transmitted to each subsequent generation. One would be hard-pressed to understand this as a negative thing.

A conservative Christian element, though, might evaluate their undertaking as ultimately pagan. The issue is not so much conservation practices as the reverence, maybe even veneration, that is accorded to created things. The earth, this group would claim, should not be an object of devotion. To do so is tantamount to idolatry. To such an accusation I can only respond with a resounding "perhaps." I suppose it is up to each participant to recognize a distinction between a means and an end. To mistake one for the other is admittedly idolatrous. Yet these participants seem not to be cognizant of such a concern.

I cannot help but think that God does not look upon these proceedings and condemn the dancers as "dirty, rotten scoundrels." At most God could charge them with being "poor, miserable wretches" who need to be shown the right path. But even this type of language may be too strong. No doubt God is pleased that some have stumbled upon a proper way to care for the land. Is that enough, however? Does this mean that they are or are not like the "despicable characters" who inhabited the land of Canaan prior to the Israelites?

At the risk of sounding anthropomorphic, if God fails to be honored by the people, then God's responses might not be unlike those found in humans. Perhaps our reactions to certain situations reveal contours of our character that have divine parallels. Like someone whose ideas are borrowed without mention, maybe God just wants an acknowledgment. To give someone due credit for something often involves a show of gratitude. Could it be that God wishes to be recognized as the provider of the bounty of the land and simply desires to be thanked for it? If this is the case, then honoring the land falls a step short of rendering due credit. Maybe this is why the God of the text is put off. I imagine we would be too. What this calls for is a realignment of focus, especially if God holds the patent or copyright.

Now reintroducing our theme, there has been criticism about the way the Israelites took over the land of Canaan. While I do not intend ever to charge God with wrongdoing or allege that God's actions are somehow morally inferior to the way others may have handled it, something does need to be said about the account as it stands. This is our opportunity to vent our frustrations.

As we mentioned, some commentators, perhaps rightly so, have considered it odd that the God of the text would at a stroke declare the righteousness of refraining from killing and then command the Israelites to drive out the nations from the land. And the way this driving out was to occur was through the extermination not only of the human inhabitants but also the domesticated animals. In fact, everything that had breath in it was to be destroyed

(Deuteronomy 7:2; 13:15; 20:16-18)—a divine ethnic cleansing together with an infra-human species cleansing. The reason given for this harsh treatment is the wickedness on the part of the then current inhabitants for their idolatrous ways (Deuteronomy 9:4-5) and so that Israel would not adopt those practices (12:29-31). God could not countenance their ways, so they were to be shown no mercy (7:2).

Who knows if the Israelites had the same vengeful spirit so that God's directive would have resonated with them. After just having narrowly escaped from Pharaoh and the Egyptians, maybe they did not see themselves as in a position to negotiate with the divine lawgiver. In defense of the Canaanites, could they not have been warned to amend their ways as the Ninevites were in the book of the prophet Jonah and who responded with obedience? Could an appeal not have been made for them also to follow the law of God? I admit that wisdom fails me here. Some might take solace in the view that annihilation was a warranted divine plan B, but then it could be asked if plan A was too hastily aborted. After all, we are the ones who are supposed to have trouble showing mercy, not God.

Early on in my educational training, the difference between envy and jealousy was impressed upon me. The former indicates a desire on the part of the one experiencing this emotion for what another person has or is, in terms of property, possession or status. In contradistinction, the latter refers to an emotion directed toward an individual or group who has received the attention of another person or community for which the first person was vying. When the Judeo-Christian scriptures speak of emotional responses on the part of the divinity, it is only the latter of these two which is in view. God never displays envy, since the deity is understood as not deficient in anything, something which no creature can boast. Of the two, only jealousy applies to God.

God's jealousy and anger are aroused when the Israelites pay homage to something other than God. These may take the form of wood, stone or metal, and they may be shaped in the form of an animal, person, or something within the already existing creation.

The difficulty lies in the fact that these images might also represent some principality or power or celestial body which the devotee has chosen in place of the Hebrew divinity (Exodus 20:3-6). And God objects to this offense of devotion to graven images. God not only reserves the term idolatry for such practices but even refers to it as prostitution.

God insists on having no rivals to compete with, for the issue revolves around divided loyalties on the part of the nation of Israel. As one partner is grieved when there is infidelity on the part of the other, so God is enraged over the waywardness and wanderings of the "chosen people." God wants their hearts, but they have given it to something else. Jealousy rightfully describes the resulting emotion on God's part.

There is also a list of items which, according to the accounts, the God of the text judges as detestable practices. These include divination and sorcery, as well as consulting mediums and spiritists (Leviticus 19: 26-31). Casting spells and engaging in witchcraft are further roundly forbidden (Deuteronomy 18:9-13), and for which the perpetrator must pay the ultimate penalty (Exodus 22:18). The sacred texts of the Jews and Christians do not deny that these practices occur. Saul, the first king of Israel, for example, seeks the assistance of a witch so as to consult the spirit of the dead prophet Samuel (1Samuel 28). The possibility exists, but God rejects the practice.

One question that could be raised in response to the foregoing is which injunctions of the Old Testament are intended for all times and places and which, if any, are meant only for the era in which they were drafted? It appears that no amount of time could ever erase the offense which the divinity would have toward idolatry. God will countenance no competitors. Would the same, however, apply to the other concerns? For instance, the stipulation to do no work on the Sabbath is an item on the list of the Ten Commandments, which also includes the rejection of idolatry and for which there were severe punishments. Perhaps all ten are not to be understood as permanent or stated with equal emphasis. Certainly the law forbidding work on the Sabbath has, it would seem, become relaxed since that time. The apostle Paul (presumably) in Romans 14: 5 informs us that issues such as these are left up to the individual conscience, an idea that would have been abhorrent to the early Judaic priesthood with its belief that there is a law for every occasion.

So how is one to know which practices, if any, no longer come under the same condemnation? There are those who would contend that all of them still apply. Both sides, it is likely, cannot be equally correct. To what extent, then, are these scriptures to constitute a complete and final word? Over the course of time, does God lighten up or continue to go by the book? Or do humans mature so that they can be entrusted with more responsibility? If the relaxation on the part of Sabbath regulations is any indication, for each of the Abrahamic traditions supports a different holy day—chronologically Saturday for Jews, Sunday for Christians and Friday for Muslims—then the divinity may entertain breadth with the passage of time as followers themselves broaden. This at least is my hope.

Injecting

> *Leviticus 14:34—When you come into the land of Canaan, which I give you for a possession, and I put a [spreading mildew in a house in that land (NIV—New International Version)],...*

We have been taught not to look a gift horse in the mouth. What this means, I suppose, is that if we are given a gift, we should not examine it with critical eyes to determine if it meets our exacting standards. It is a gift after all. One who receives a gift should not be like a merchant who scrutinizes an item for purposes of deciding whether or not to invest in it. Yet some gifts we can do without. We would like to think that those who send something our way have our best interests at heart. Some gifts, however, do more harm than good. It would have been better had the sender refrained from introducing the item into our lives.

The sacred texts of the Judeo-Christian tradition teach that this also applies, brace yourselves, to the God of the text. God does not always act in our best interests. The passage above states that at times God *places* a destructive mildew in the houses of the children of Israel. Nowhere in the text does it claim that this condition is brought about as a response to disobedience on the part of the home-owners. There is no indication of the existence of a one-to-one correspondence between worthiness and freedom from microbial attack. The lifestyle of the home-owner does not appear to be at issue.

Mildew is not a respecter of persons. Neither, we could surmise, is the God who sends it. This leaves us mystified about the rationale on God's part as to who gets to deal with this blight, which could result in the destruction of all or part of the affected homes. In such cases, the priest was dispatched to investigate the mildew and the procedure which God outlined called for uncovering whether it is a spreading mildew. If so, it was diagnosed as destructive. The prescription was for scraping those stones showing signs of mildew and isolating the house for one week so as to disclose if the spread had been forestalled. Failing that, the offending stones were to be removed from the house and taken outside the camp into a secure spot. Seemingly, even the Israelites dealt with hazardous materials and assigned an area as a toxic dump.

Another passage of scripture might illumine us on our path of concern as to what to make of the current one. Isaiah 45:7 instructs us that God not only fashions the light but also creates darkness, brings weal (prosperity) as well as woe (disaster). We would be inclined to view ordinary individuals in a negative light if they behaved this way and would not normally consider God as subject to what we would usually appraise as human foibles and frailties. What the passage intends is that all of creation is under God's command and it employs a poetic device of listing opposites so as to imply the totality in order to make its point. But it remains the case that darkness and disaster are well within the divine comfort zone and not foreign to God's method of operation. That which the insurance companies term "acts of God" might in fact have scriptural warrant. The text informs us as to what its God is capable of. (As an aside, there are even parts of scripture that are "unsuitable for all audiences" and reader "discretion is strongly advised." An example of a passage that would earn a Restricted rating is Ezekiel 23:20.)

The text also reminds us that "Every generous act of giving, with every perfect gift, is from above, coming down from the Father of lights,..." (James 1:17). What it neglects to mention is that not all gifts are good. In the Leviticus and Isaiah verses above, not everyone received from God's hands what was beneficial. Does this diminish God's goodness and love? No, it just places it in a different perspective. We might have been working all along with a vending machine type of divinity filled with goodies and ready to dispense them upon request. Wherever we got this idea, it was not from the text. God continues to be generous, but is not above dishing out some bumps or beyond "bringing it." God has muscle as well as compassion. There is wisdom in the writing of Ecclesiastes, where in chapter three a list of earthly occurrences is compiled along with a statement as to how each can be seen as opportune. There is a time for killing and healing because God participates in both. There is a time for loving and hating because God expresses both. (Here are some of the things that God hates, according to the accounts: robbery (Isaiah 61:8); divorce (Malachi 2:16); even Esau (Malachi 1:3); and an additional list of seven (Proverbs 6:16-19).) There is a time for war and peace because God has been known both to engage in the former and promote the latter. This marks yet another complex tension we are called upon to live with. Thankfully, God's mercy outweighs the negative aspects in each case, else we would not be around to state an objection.

The Wedding

Isaiah 62:5—For as a young man marries a young woman, so shall your builder marry you, and as the bridegroom rejoices over the bride, so shall your God rejoice over you.

Opposites attract, apparently. This is most clearly observed in electromagnetism where like charges repel and unlike charges attract. When conditions are dry, two persons can be exposed to a startling display of affection when static electricity interferes with the intimacy of osculation. (No pain, no gain, I suppose.) Couples may differ widely in physical features. Cathy Rigby, diminutive U.S. gymnast, is said to have wed a beau very tall in comparison. There can also be a diversity of psychological characteristics in couples, from demeanor and deportment to idiosyncrasies. This makes for the association of individuals into potentially numerous odd couples, which might defy any type of logic, thereby prompting us to exclaim that love is blind and romance is irrational.

What attracts them to each other may in fact be their contrast, the novelty of their otherness, which might complement their own character traits. Yet the strength of relationships could very well come from what couples hold in common—possibly their interests, expectations and values. This commonality is what I wish to focus on presently.

Seemingly, humans are not the only ones who find other humans attractive. According to the accounts, the God of the biblical text courts a certain nation—the Hebrews then Jews of the Old Testament and later the Christian Church in the New. It is not always clear what attracts couples to each other, but God apparently sees something God likes, and so pursues it. The record of the relationship sometimes is expressed in vivid nuptial language, where God is the bridegroom and Israel and the Church (the new Israel) is the bride (Psalms 19:5; and Revelation 21:2 as additional examples).

I have wondered what it was or is that attracts the divinity to a chosen people so that the latter might become the betrothed. It cannot be because Israel and the Church are so like God, for the differences are striking. Yet it is useful to take stock so as to ensure an enduring relationship. Beauty can be fleeting, so there must needs be more substance to it. Hence in the biblical case, what can one learn about God from the relationship that God wishes to enter? At first glance, it is clear that the mate God has found has priorities other than godliness. No sense, then, looking for commonality amongst interests, goals and values. Despite recognizing this, perhaps God envisions what the bride can become and is willing to draw this out of the beloved. God seems to be prepared to undergo the heartache of a groom countenancing a bride who is given to infidelity, all for the prospect of receiving a more refined product in the end. This informs us that the God of the text is long-suffering, exhibiting patient endurance that the bride return. As mentioned, the character qualities exemplifying God are usually lacking in the bride, so the attraction is not based on high mutual regards. But this does not propel God into seeking a more suitable and compatible companion. God is not irretrievably repelled by the bride but sticks to a commitment, come what may, even if it means sending the partner away for a time to refocus and detoxify. Or, witnessing their plight in Pharaoh's Egypt for instance, God likes cheering for the underdog.

Jesting (or Facetious Jesus)

The Jesus portrayed in the gospels could be viewed as the rough equivalent of a Jon Stewart of his day, not least in the way that both of them happen to be Jewish. As the host of his own comedy/talk show called the Daily Show, Jon Stewart is a liberal-minded pseudo news broadcaster who pokes fun at the misguided policies and antics of the recent (G.W. Bush) U.S. administration. While other topics are also the target of his satire, a conservative government is most often in his cross-hairs. There always seems to be ample comedic fodder with political criticism, making for an entertaining program. Jesus could be understood in somewhat similar terms. He would have been seen as a liberal, if not an outright radical, in his day, at least in comparison with the religious leaders at the time. These were the Pharisees, who themselves were liberal compared to the group known as the Sadducees.

This latter collective was of the conservative mindset that theology is to be drawn entirely from the Torah—the five books ascribed to Moses (the first five books of the Bible, namely Genesis, Exodus, Leviticus, Numbers and Deuteronomy). No other writings, in their eyes, were to be accorded the same sacred status as these five. Nothing in terms of the Psalms, for example, part of what are referred to as the Wisdom writings, had the same significance for them. They confined their theology to the message Moses (allegedly) had to convey. If it was not contained in these writings, it could be safely bypassed.

The same could not be said for the Pharisees. What they took to be sacred text was not limited to the "writings" of Moses. They were a broader thinking bunch, as can be seen when, for instance, debates surrounding the resurrection arose. For the Sadducees, the issue was quite straightforward. Nothing of the sort appeared, so they surmised, in the Torah, so they resolved to dispense with the question. Not so for the Pharisees. They detected passages such as Daniel 12:1-2, which in their estimation spoke to the concern. Hence for them it was a live theme and led to heated discussions with their counterparts. (The apostle Paul, who was on trial before the Sanhedrin—the religious judicial council, in Acts 23:6-10—strategically used this dispute to divert the attention away from himself.)

Then along comes this Jesus character who out-liberals even the Pharisees and makes them out to be the legalistic types they were. Like a true stand-up comic he was quick with a comeback, leaving his critics speechless. When the Pharisees, who emphasize adherence to the law and ritual purity, approached Jesus with the complaint that his disciples were eating heads of grain from a field on the Sabbath, Jesus immediately recalled the episode of king David—a hero of the faith whom the Pharisees also held in high regard—when he did what was unlawful in eating consecrated bread. And this is to say nothing of the temple priesthood that is always employed with impunity on the Sabbath (Matthew 12:1-8) when no work is to be done.

The Pharisees further contended that Jesus was able to drive out demons only through demonic power, to which he replied, "What would be the sense of that? Would not Satan then be working at cross-purposes?" (Mark 3:23-26). Moreover, when asked why he and his disciples do not wash their hands before they eat, in accordance with the tradition, Jesus responded with "more importantly, why do you not honor your father and mother?—a more valuable tradition" (Matthew 15:1-9) (paraphrasing in both cases).

Returning for a moment to the topic of the Sadducees and the resurrection, the gospel accounts (Matthew 22:23-33 and the parallels in Mark 12:18-27 and Luke 20:27-40) depict Jesus as confronted by this group with a question designed to force Jesus into an awkward philosophical position. If he is committed to a view similar to that of the Pharisees, they argue, then he will find this puzzle embarrassing. They hypothesize that a man marries a woman but then dies, and according to custom the brother who is next in line must marry the woman and produce offspring for the now deceased brother. The Sadducees propose that the same thing occurred to this brother, and continued all the way down the line until the last of seven brothers married her and died. Whose wife will she be at the resurrection?, they ask, for all were married to her. Jesus replies by claiming that the Sadducees are in error for they know neither the scriptures nor the power of God. Firstly, the risen dead do not marry for they are like the angelic beings. Secondly, Exodus 3:15 has it that God's response to Moses' question, as to whom shall he say sent him back to Egypt to liberate the Israelites, was that the God of Moses' ancestors sends him— the God of Abraham, Isaac and Jacob. Since the present tense is employed, therefore God *is*, not *was*, their God. Jesus interprets this to mean that God is the God of the living, not the dead. This prompts Jesus to infer that the patriarchs are alive to God. The clincher is that the Exodus passage is located in the only part of the scriptures which the Sadducees recognize as authoritative. Have another look, Jesus implies. Your own sacred text attests to the resurrection.

Yet I do not find this line of thinking conclusive. The use of the present tense is a literary device, thereby not to be taken literally. But judging by the way the account ends, it suggests that the Sadducees might have been trumped. The Matthean version has the crowd astonished at Jesus' teaching and the Lukan rendition has some of the scribes (lawyers) congratulating Jesus for his oratorical skills. While the content of Jesus' counterpoint is not strictly a comedic rib-tickler or knee-slapper, his response evidently generated nods of approval from his hearers.

A similar result could have been obtained in the immediately preceding passage in each of the three synoptic gospels cited. There Jesus is pressured into choosing between allegiance to the Law or to Rome in the form of paying taxes to Caesar. Another trap was set for him. Inclining in either direction would have disastrous repercussions. If he decided in favor of one, he would become the enemy of the other in the eyes of the people. In his wisdom he elected to display a Roman coin and asserted that the proper place for coins is in the hands of those responsible for minting them, whereas the payment of homage is rightly reserved for God: "Give to Caesar what is Caesar's and to God what is God's." According to the accounts, the people were amazed and marvelled at his rejoinder. Jesus sure knew how to work a crowd.

One of the most unfunny things to do is to analyze a joke and explain what made it witty. This occurs in Matthew 16:5-12, where Jesus makes a quip about the teaching of the Pharisees as being like yeast that makes dough rise. The disciples had forgotten to take bread along on a journey across the lake, so Jesus cautions them to watch out for the leaven of the Pharisees—that is, not to let it work on you like yeast in dough. They didn't get it. After Jesus likely wiped his face with his hand in disbelief and cried out the Aramaic equivalent of "Oh, brother," he explained the pun. But it was too late to get a "rise" out of his audience. (Pardon this pun. These plays on words are likely the only form of witticism for which a pardon is sought.)

The Jesus of the text was also not above name-calling, for he referred to Herod as a fox (Luke 13:31-32), certain that this would have had poignancy at the time. I guess you had to be there. Jesus could very well have been the host of his own talk show, where he would have inflicted jabs on the ruling establishment, both political and religious. The programming, though, might not have lasted long, since it could have been pulled early on for lack of political and religious correctness. Some people just can't take a joke.

Characterizing

Humans are curious creatures. At times they will entertain ideas that in other instances they themselves might judge as counter-intuitive or lacking substance. There are authors who recognize this and have tapped into what they consider to be a rich resource or fertile field. Dan Brown *(The DaVinci Code)* comes to mind. He sees something that could lead to the temptation known as a conspiracy theory. For those addicted to this narcotic, it is a trap easily fallen into. Here is how Brown accomplishes it.

There is a long tradition that understands Jesus to be celibate, even sinless (not that the two are connected). Regardless of the truth or falsehood of these claims, this is not the issue for certain propagandists. If a convincing argument can be brought forward that sheds a less than complimentary light on an alleged high and mighty personage, then readers will tend to focus their attention on such a tidbit. Multiple cliches are applicable here: one bad apple... like a fly in the ointment..., as examples. The latter saying, incidentally, stems from Ecclesiastes 10:1. The extended quote is: "As dead flies give perfume a bad smell, so a little folly outweighs wisdom and honor." People seem to enjoy knowing that a reputation has been tarnished. What better victim than a guy who some call divine? This makes good copy and Brown knows it. He becomes a prosecuting attorney and his writings take on a tabloid aroma.

He identifies, apparently with the help of others, a break from tradition which strikes a responsive chord with certain opponents of it. Brown locates in Leonardo da Vinci's painting of the Last Supper a potentially embarrassing feature. The figure to Jesus' right can be interpreted as not a male disciple but a female, which Brown claims is no less than Mary Magdalene, who was in fact Jesus' consort. So much for celibacy.

This kind of story is tantalizing. It is astounding how one piece of evidence can outweigh a wealth of contrary reports. More significantly, the news is taken on a par with the other, that is, the data secured from da Vinci is assumed to be of the same caliber as the entirety of the tradition that preceded it. Regardless of how one evaluates the biblical witness, it is a longstanding one which ought to receive a hearing at least for its seniority. Da Vinci is not a historian, theologian or biblical scholar, yet both his works and the tradition being scrutinized are seen as equally authoritative, with the nod given to the lone exhibit—a painting containing an item potentially damaging to the tradition—having the greatest entertainment value. If only the first biblical documents came with illustrations!

But there are some additional data to examine. Most notably, da Vinci is a critic of the religious establishment. He has no intention of having his products faithfully reflect sacred tradition. Not only does he place his own stamp on his artwork, he creates a caricature. Make people wonder if Jesus' right hand man is actually a woman. This is how he wishes to drive his point home. In the realm of authentic history, he is a cartoonist. And with a promoter like Dan Brown, da Vinci gains a following. Perhaps da Vinci's contemporaries did not get the joke. Nor did we—something Brown was banking on. We are no closer to uncovering the actual events than we were before. Brown made us believe, however, that we are. We have been had. It can be assessed—both for readers of sacred texts as well as for the tabloids—that we are quick to believe the sensational. This tells us more about our own makeup than perhaps we are willing to divulge.

As an addendum to the foregoing, Michael Baigent—one of the authors of *Holy Blood, Holy Grail*, who claimed that Dan Brown drew from their ideas when preparing his *Da Vinci Code*—in his recent solo offering entitled *The Jesus Papers* discloses another tasty treat, once again from a painting. One of the Stations of the Cross in a church in southern France includes a painting of a wounded but living Jesus being transported on a moonlit night, suggesting that Jesus' crucifixion did not end in death, but that the death was actually staged. Baigent uses this interpretation as a basis on which to build his case. The notion of such a concocted story is not new, but this painting adds fuel to the fire, or at least stokes the embers. Here is another instance in which an argument depends on the attractiveness or even seductiveness of one item over against many others.

The tradition, which Baigent seeks to overturn, for what it is worth, delivers multiple attestations for Jesus' death, burial and resurrection. Granted, the gospels are not the best place to look for negative reports about Jesus. Admittedly, as history is written by the victors, so biographies are often (though not always) crafted by admirers. Give the Pharisees and Sadducees a pen and parchment and they would draft a different account. Jesus would then not be made to look like a hero. Not possessing such offerings, we are left with documents that view Jesus in the best possible light. Each version would contain its biases and agenda. The gospels are no exception. This applies also to those artistic representations adduced by Brown and Baigent that came much later.

The contrary evidence may be slim, but this does not bother the intrepid conspiracy theorist. Nothing sells copy like something charged with scandal. Like Fox Mulder in the *X-Files*, people want to believe this type of news. Some authors endeavor to ensure that enough of it is around. The odd thing is that if other cases were attempted to be grounded on such flimsy evidence, they would be laughed out of court. I invite the reader to attempt to gain the same kind of support with the paucity of evidence for, say, the miraculous. What s/he would be up against is the resistance toward accepting something that most schools of thought frown upon at best and reject at worst. Slim evidence works for conspiracies but not miracles (outside of visions of and crying statues of the Virgin Mary in Catholic circles). One wonders why, but then it becomes clear. The current naturalistic, as opposed to super-naturalistic mindset, of course, stands in the way. A materialist mentality will not allow it. Yet the inconsistency is staggering, though understandable. Both instances—a Jesus who survived the crucifixion and the rejection of the miraculous—are of the same type, for the former amounts to a recourse for rejecting another miracle. These spirits are kindred.

Confirming

John 16:5-13—Unless I go away, the Advocate [or Counselor (NIV)]
will not come to you; but if I go, I will send him to you...When the Spirit
of truth comes, he will guide you into all the truth...

Amen. May it be so. What this passage does not divulge, however,
is the time element involved, which appears to be in two stages.
First, if there can be confidence in the time-line given in John's
gospel, Jesus uttered these words on the eve of his arrest. This
leaves three days for the trial, crucifixion, death and resurrection,
plus fifty days until Pentecost when the spirit was poured out onto
the disciples in the upper room (Acts 2). That makes fifty-three
days for the fulfilment of the first part of the announcement. As for
the second, we are still waiting. Much like the disciples anticipated
a speedy return on Christ's part subsequent to his ascension, they
had to regroup theologically and make the necessary adjustments
when it did not occur immediately. We are given no indication as
to the schedule of communication of this truth, that is, when the
informational transaction is to take place. Issues certainly began
to become clarified in due course, at least to the minds of the
disciples. For them the spirit assisted them in their exegesis and
hermeneutics—making sense of the words of Jesus and the eventual biblical text. (This can be seen as early as Luke's gospel where
the risen Jesus walked with two disciples on the road to Emmaus
and explained to them the meaning of the scriptures concerning
himself (24: 13-27). But that, of course, is the risen Jesus and not
the promised Spirit.)
    This is not the end of the story. With time there also surfaced
additional issues for which the spiritual leaders needed to recon-
vene so as to come, if possible, to a consensus. Often prompted
by what came to strike them as erroneous ideas and movements,
the church ultimately took a stand in opposition to these ideas in
order to distinguish their views from others. They then regarded
their own position as orthodox (right belief) and those of others
as heterodoxical, unorthodox, or outright heretical. As has so often been recognized, the victors get to write history and call the

vanquished (at best) the misguided or deluded, or (at worst) in league with the devil.

Hence there is an evolution of doctrine. When issues came to light that required a ruling, a court of appeal was established, usually in the form of a church council. It would be nice to describe the events therein as proceeding from muddiness to clarity, but such is not always the case. Apparently, the spirit was not completed with the truth program in the aftermath of Pentecost. Many further questions needed to be settled. Over the centuries, the church took a stand on a variety of theological themes such as the divinity of Christ, the Virgin Birth/Immaculate Conception, the Trinity and creatio ex nihilo (creation from nothing). Evidently the leading into truth needed time to simmer.

Thus the problems are still not overcome; the work is unfinished. There are differences of opinion even within the same tradition, what can be called "in-house debates." On occasion, the differences became so pronounced that they engendered a parting of the ways. There were a number of splits and schisms which arose to divide the one catholic church. It would seem that the truth does not always unify. This of course is not a new thing. In the early days of the church, discussions about evangelistic strategy and personnel became so heated that the apostle Paul joined forces with Silas while parting company with Barnabas and Mark (Acts 15:36-41), though we could safely assume that the same Spirit was operative in all four. Consequently, the presence and assistance of the spirit of truth does not automatically prevent contrary views or even "sharp disagreements" in doctrine or methodology from occurring between even those in the same camp.

This continued throughout the history of Christendom and remains a concern into the present. The Protestant movement is famous for this formal fragmentation (pardon the alliteration). Each time doctrinal disputes become elevated to critical status, a new association pinches off from its parent and takes on a life and name of its own. So where is the truth? Reform movements continue to emerge, since the church could always do with a little renovation. This is why the church continues to reform itself.

Cleaning house is never complete, nor is a theologian's work ever done. Theological advancements continue to be made, although not everyone would agree that they amount to improvements.

The additional difficulty is that equally devout participants in the various debates can be found on opposite sides of the fence. Which one has the truth? Is the spirit operative in one but not the other? Or perhaps there is a little truth in each? Even the apostle Paul affirms that "Indeed there have to be factions among you, for only so will it become clear who among you are genuine" (1 Corinthians 11:19). (Another version has it that "No doubt there have to be differences among you to show which of you have God's approval" [NIV—New International Version].) What is more, is a resolution to an issue ultimately a matter of truth? Theological brothers and sisters may squabble but they are still part of the same family. Filial relationship is not threatened. Brothers do not cease to be brothers simply because they fight. Truth might not reside solely in the accurate formulation of concepts but also in the alliance of the heart. The main concern may be not so much doctrinal precision in particular as an avoidance of idolatry in general. The spirit of truth, in my estimation, is interested in preventing a decline toward the worship of false gods—something to which we are all prone. And this can occur inside as well as outside of "the camp." Leading into truth perhaps begins with a turning from what is false.

Despite their best efforts, it did not take long before they got it wrong. After only about one generation, when the followers of the Way (which is what the movement was originally named) began to organize what they thought about the nascent faith, they fell wide of the mark in at least one regard. More on this below, but first a word about biographies and biographers. As there is both a continuity and a discontinuity in beliefs from one testament to the next, the writer(s) of Matthew's gospel endeavored to argue with many references as to how the old view was fulfilled in Jesus. But there came to be a disjunct between Jesus' message and the disciples' interpretation of it. As they made the attempt to strike a continuity between the traditional Jewish faith and the transformation Jesus hoped to inspire in it, the movement evolved so as to become an incipient faith, complete with its own understanding and expectations. Matthew's gospel, for example, emphasized the continuity of Jesus in the Jewish tradition by importing passages from the Hebrew scriptures (prior to their being referred to by Christians as the Old Testament), to demonstrate how they related to the new situation. One wonders, though, if Jesus would have had this self-understanding. Would he have recognized himself in any gospel depiction of him? And four gospels yielded four different versions of Jesus' life and ministry, not all of which can be true in their entirety.

Before any canonical gospels were committed to writing, the apostle Paul wrote letters to fledgling congregations. Whether intended or not, these missives became equal in standing to the scriptures that came before them. And with time, these letters also assumed, or were accorded, the status of scripture themselves along with other writings. During the period of Paul's literary output, the mood appeared to be, as mentioned above, one of anticipation of Jesus' imminent return. This sentiment is echoed even in what is understood as one of the latest writings of that which became the New Testament, namely the book of Revelation. There both the initial and final passages refer to events that "must soon take place," "for the time is near," and on a few occasions reference is made to Jesus, the Lamb, as "coming soon" (Revelation 1:1, 3; 3:11; 22:7, 12, 20). Evidently, from our perspective, this is a meaning of "soon" that we are not normally accustomed to hold. For in contrast to the anticipation of the first generation of believers, it would seem that God is not in a hurry. God is not stressed about meeting our timetables, nor are we adept at uncovering God's. Our schedules are not at the forefront of God's agenda.

Hence the initial attempt to structure the tenets of this new faith faltered, and this at the heels of the promise that the spirit would lead into the truth. That leading, presumably, does not guarantee the circumvention of our penchant to think and reason falsely. In actuality, the crafting of all theologies is fraught with difficulties and inaccuracies. They can still be offerings of worship to God—even pleasing sacrifices—but they are not unblemished.

The God of the Old Testament who is stated as not accepting blemished temple sacrifices appears less stern in the New. God seems to appreciate the attempt, warts and all. Our focus, naturally, must be to strive for ever more acceptable sacrifices, but this does not diminish God's pleasure at receiving sincere offerings. Not every one can be a blue ribbon entry, but this may not be of prime importance to God. What matters most is a heart tuned in to God's frequency or wavelength. Even though it is possible to be sincere but in error, God judges the intentions of the heart (see for example 1 Samuel 16:7 and Hebrews 4:12). Refinements are pending.

Besides, given the historical results, it must be admitted, if we are honest, that perhaps in us the spirit is not working with the brightest of bulbs. One issue could be our inability to sense the spirit's prompting as well as our failure to recognize and comprehend its message. The lines of communication are sometimes faulty and the reception blurred.

Returning to the book of Revelation, one can ask what kind of God is portrayed there. Chapters four and five paint the picture of the heavenly throne where God is surrounded by a multitude of worshipers, both angelic and human. The image I receive when reflecting on these passages is of a concert where the entertainer has completed his or her artistic set and is being showered with applause from the audience. God's creativity, for which God is being hailed as paramount, is the making of everything new—the renewal of creation. Using the concert analogy, God has in effect brought the house down and is receiving from the throng a standing (or flying?) ovation that will never end. This was a show-stopper and the witnesses are voicing their appreciation. God only knows if there will be an encore performance.

Selecting

Every vocation has its joys and sorrows, its highlights and hardships. I am grateful for the duties that I have been given to perform, one of which is an instructional task at the college level.

The bulk of my obligations there are enlivening. Little in my life can match the elation of witnessing the great "aha" experience when a new thought dawns and is driven home in the minds of class members. If discoveries like this are taken to heart, lives can become transformed and I consider it a privilege to facilitate the process.

One of my least enjoyable activities, however, in this otherwise fulfilling undertaking, is the grading of written submissions. I point out that the Bible teaches that we should not judge, lest we be judged (Matthew 7:1; Luke 6:37), yet the college administration is unmoved by this argument. So here we are evaluating the work of others. The obligation to judge is needful for a society to govern itself. In an educational setting, it is warranted for the assessment of abilities. Thankfully, sometimes there are teaching assistants to whom this task is assigned. Having been employed as one on occasion, I am glad to have paid my dues and passed the reins on to someone else.

When I am called upon to grade, it quickly becomes evident that there are a range of talents on the part of those submitting papers. Some are more capable than others. Some can articulate and argue a point cogently; others have difficulty. In each class there are those essays which display high technical and artistic quality. Encountering these makes the job of grading worthwhile.

It was not until recently when another "aha" experience surfaced, this time extending to me. The process itself came up for review: writings, papers, good points, poorer points, higher and lower quality, convincing arguments, opinion and fluff. Hey, wait a moment. Could this be applied to the documents that emerged as the New Testament? There were a collection of writings in the initial century (or two, or three) of the Christian or Common Era, some of which had better points and higher quality than others. But which to select as definitive? What to do, what to do?

Those who gathered in early church councils could be considered the T.A.s who graded the papers. They came together to compare notes. The conversation could have proceeded something like this: "These ones deserve a higher grade; we seem to be in agreement on this. We declare which should be those to stand as final contestants on 'Mediterranean Idol' or 'So You Think You Can Witness?'" Hence ecclesiastical T.A.s graded the writings which would soon become scripture. The judges decided, for instance, that these four gospels, for better or for worse, shall remain from among all the other candidates. The others do not make the grade. The bar has been elevated to this height and most do not measure up.

The documents were judged on the basis of their ability to inspire the readers to hear God's call. The churches agreed that these were the most enduring ones. Different T.A.s will evaluate differently, though. There is no instructor available to act as ultimate arbiter, however, and this is where the analogy breaks down. All need to rely on wisdom and the spirit's leading ("it seemed good to the Holy Spirit and to us" (Acts 15:28), which makes this a collaborative effort). Yet we noticed in the previous selections that this is not a straightforward task. Thus consensus is not always an attainable goal. The final choice should therefore not be regarded as a reflection of these writings as holding a monopoly on spiritual insight. Other writings might contain a certain amount of it too. But the graders were given, or assumed, the authorization to decide which ones were to be conferred canonical status, and these decisions affected all the readers who came afterward. The accepted writings became the standard of how the faith was to be understood and practised.

Those that did not pass muster can still exhibit value of their own, which some may have overlooked. And since that time still other writings have come to light which call for our attention. How the faith might have been altered had these other and additional documents been chosen alongside the authorized ones!

The selection process reflects the concerns of the time period in which the documents find themselves. But does this make them permanently binding? The church through the ages confirmed that these writings possess great spiritual merit, yet does that mean the canon should remain forever closed? As students have bemoaned since evaluations of this sort began,"it depends on who grades it."

It has been my good fortune to be able to go public with some of these views. In the process, students have submitted term papers which on occasion included resources from class discussion. Sometimes the material thus cited bore only a partial resemblance to what actually transpired. Those cases left me bewildered as to whether I or someone else misspoke—entirely within the realm of possibility—or the student simply misheard. If it was the latter case, and if this represents a not unknown potentiality on the part of hearers, then perhaps this might also be the case in other circumstances, such as with sacred texts. Humans have been known to miscommunicate—one need only be reminded of the broken telephone effect where a message at the end of a long line of human transmitters bears little resemblance to the original—meaning the scriptures may also bear the marks of faulty communication. With good reason the Bible refers to the workman who correctly explains or handles the word of truth (2 Timothy 2:15), for this appears to be a requirement for each generation. Hence precision of communication is not automatic, particularly if there are third parties, or more, involved.

Much like the blind men who, unbeknownst to them, examine an elephant, each claiming that s/he has hit upon what the full account is—some insisting that the object must be a tree, having felt the sturdiness of the legs, while others that it must be a snake, given the flexibility of the trunk—so theologians might each have partially captured a piece of the divine puzzle. There is distortion at each level—a given when humans are involved, as well as perhaps even the illusion that the part is entirely representative of the whole. At the very least, this ought to caution us against the hubris of infallible/inerrant interpretation.

I certainly have difficulties with the text and quarrel with it at a number of points. Now do these misgivings on my part reflect poorly on the text or the interpreter or both? In my appraisal, both scripture and theology (which is systematic reflection on those scriptures) suffer from faulty interpretation. Even the biblical accounts themselves come pre-interpreted by their authors and do not offer an unbiased presentation of the events recorded. The drafting of biographies is not without subjectivity—the infiltration of personal preference—and there is no such thing as an uninterpreted account. I am not, nor do I feel the need to be, committed to the view that these words amount to a complete depiction of the deity, as though this were a prerequisite for admission either to the Christian community or God's grace. To my thinking the text is less an owner's manual for the faith than a travel log on the part of some of the faithful. We are not left on our own, for the Spirit is there to assist and to guide, otherwise the impression is given that God has been silent and inactive for two thousand years. But issues are not as certain as we might like. They remain subject to the Spirit's unveiling. And God only knows how closely they and the sacred text approximate the divine communique.

Distressing

Taking a more topical approach, allow me to address a most thorny issue—the theodicy problem, otherwise known as the problem of evil. This treatment must, for our purposes, be cursory, but I would be remiss if I did not at least mention it.

Detectives and law enforcement agencies are involved in the search for what motivates persons to commit crimes. Theologians, too, have motives for the work they undertake. They are not customarily associated with a criminal element, though on occasion critics of their work might be inclined to describe their systematic formulations in those terms. At the risk of oversimplifying, a motivating factor which I detect on the part of theologians who draft proposals on the nature of God sometimes takes the shape of what to do with the perplexing issue of God's justice—a justification of the ways of God. The motivation on the part of certain theologians may very well turn on how to clear God of the charge of any wrongdoing—as if God requires our services in this matter. An act of God perceived as outside the confines of acceptable behavior, whether divine or human, might also be interpreted as a derailment of all that God stands for. God's honor, after all, is at stake. The difficulty is in determining what is at fault here—God's standards or ours.

The pursuit is a noble and commendable one. A God who is open to the charge of injustice is not worth following. Hence theologians become pressed into the service of advocacy—defending God's strategy against all accusers. "Be not hasty in finger-pointing," they might implore us. "God's ways are higher than ours, so acquiesce and let God be God. No one else is qualified to do the job." The task is completed when apologists are able to supply us with sophisticated philosophical argumentation as to how God's justice remains unsullied and God's honor intact. There are times when, by the end of their treatise, if indeed we can remember the question, that we are sorry we asked.

Sometimes the efforts of these theologians may involve a reformulation of the concept of God so as to make their defense more effective. "We have been barking up the wrong divinity all along," they might be prompted to announce. The resolution becomes one of offering up a different view of God for our approval. Simply propose a God with an alternate complexion and *modus operandi* and the problem goes away. Why did we not think of it before? We could kick ourselves for not securing the patent or copyright first.

Not to spoil the festivities, there is, however, the consideration of the cost-benefit ratio. Everything comes at a price. What is the cost of a theological Alka-Seltzer that will calm our insides? To take one example, the process thought of Alfred North Whitehead and his followers appears to be motivated by just such a strategy. Whitehead himself was angry at God for having taken his son away from him in the First World War. The system he drew up was his attempt to come to terms with this tragedy. He could not countenance the traditional understanding of God, for the implication was that this God should have prevented it, so he crafted the only version of God that he could live with. The general formulation of arguments against God on the basis of evil tend to run this way:

Premise one: There is evil in the world.

Premise two: A good God would be willing to do something about it.

Premise three: A powerful God would be ready and able to do so.

Premise four: Evil persists; it continues unabated; there is no apparent diminution of it.

Conclusion: Therefore, a God that goes by the above description does not exist.

Compelling, no doubt. Several philosophers and theologians have attempted to overcome the difficulty through fine adjustments of this argument. Some contend that the time frame is the concern. Evil will finally be eradicated, they insist, according to God's schedule, not our convenience. We might need to wait until the end of history for that to occur. Hence the need to heed the call for patience, since "we walk by faith, not by sight" (2 Corinthians 5:7). While this may be true, it remains unsatisfactory to some, especially Whiteheadians.

Other theorists imagine what a system would look like if the second premise above were discarded. Albeit a "live option," this is not a line of thinking that process thinkers would be willing to entertain. They would be more inclined to discount the third premise. God's goodness, not God's power, should be retained. Whiteheadians insist that theologians are mistaken when they claim that God's power has equal or greater status than God's goodness. In their view, power should be subordinated to goodness. Now, of course, this calls for an elaborate reconfiguring of systematic theology for it to be coherent. So let's try it on for size.

One advantage of Whitehead's system is that it has a clear response to the problem of evil. Here is how it is accomplished. God harmonizes value possibilities such as truth, beauty and goodness for the common good. God presents these as ideals for entities to grasp. Whatever does not fall in line with this harmonious presentation is evaluated as evil. For consciousness-bearers like us, to militate against the harmony, which is God's aesthetic appeal, is to perpetrate certain forms of evil. This, of course, assumes that the level of self-determining power which humans possess is incapable of promoting the good in the absence of God's influence. What this means, I suppose, is that humans cannot be trusted to disclose and carry out the good on their own.

Yet not all evil stems from moral choices. Creatures also contend with physical evil, as the forces of nature occasionally leave destruction in their wake. This presents us with two options. Concerning God as the source of order in the world, the first is that the inorganic realm contains greater self-determination than we are likely to give it credit. This makes both God and the world players in the natural scene. If we are unprepared to concede this point, then the other alternatives are that God's power is insufficient or God is unwilling to ward off geo-based upheavals. Some may object that the order which the world displays need not be assessed in terms of its effect on or benefit for humanity. Nature has value in its own right, regardless of any human consequences. But, for value to be maximized in the universe, which is the very goal of the process God, it would seem that God might be prompted to work toward the preservation of consciousness, for the greater the consciousness, the greater the self-determining power and the greater the capacity to exert a net effect on value. Failing in that regard would likely be viewed as counterproductive.

The genius of Whitehead's system, though, lies in its view of evolution. Whereas in standard accounts God either engages in special creation or adopts evolution for God's own purposes yet remains unaffected in the process, Whitehead incorporates the divinity into the evolutionary scheme. God also evolves, though not in a Darwinian sense. Better perhaps to say that God develops or undergoes change. The question then becomes the extent to which God not only orchestrates change but is also subject to it. This can be contrasted with the proposal of Pierre Teilhard de Chardin, who understands God as at the helm of evolution and constitutes the Omega Point, the vantage point or "center of centers" from which God draws the cosmos unto God's self. Here the world changes according to the unfolding of God's purpose, but God does not. While Teilhard's God might not be fully realized until the end, the target at which God's efforts are aimed is a specific point. This makes it a forgone conclusion as to the shape which the universe together with God will ultimately take. The world does the evolving, not the divine. Whitehead's God cannot direct but hopes for a particular future; Teilhard's God does direct and works toward a particular future, though not in detail.

Perhaps the solution lies in the degree to which God is a member of the evolutionary fraternity or merely its overarching superintendent. If the latter, then God remains the same; if the former, then we need to dispense with the idea that God is static (a God of being), for change becomes part of God's nature (a God of [predominantly] becoming). Change can then be a good thing since it derives from the nature of God. Whitehead's divinity is always adding intensity of feeling and richness of experience to God's own unfolding, which makes it a positive thing. God's change is thus always for the better, but not so for creatures. They can change in ways that detract from God's intentions. If God's ideals are rejected, then evil enters the world. God is required to inject ideals into the system in the hopes that they will be accepted, God thereby being a positive influence on the world and a benchmark for the promotion of goodness. If enough creatures heed the call, then evil diminishes. Most importantly, in the process scheme the divinity operates by persuasion and not coercion. The appeal to opt for the right thing is never more than a call. This is a fundamental limitation on God's part, though process thinkers do not see it as such. Conveniently, they prefer it this way.

It took some doing, but now that God can be understood as neither having nor wielding the power to force compliance with God's intentions, evil can be accounted for. "Why bad things happen to good people" can be explained as an entirely human matter, if it is confined to the moral arena. And God's justice remains untarnished. Glad that's over with!

But the question must be asked, "is the cost too high?" Is this really the kind of world we live in? Are we faced with a toothless divinity? Admittedly, this approach does seem to quell the fears of many, yet it still has not as yet received widespread acceptance. While the majority can most assuredly be in error, is it the minority that is on to something in this case? No doubt theological mistakes have been made and continue to be made. When attempting to debate which one trumps the other—God's goodness or power—does our judgment fail us? Despite Whitehead's proposal as an astute and complex one, does it amount simply to an easy fix? Just keep God's goodness and make God's power expendable. A straightforward resolution, though the way to get there is not.

Since we are dealing with a divinity, we ought to give God more credit than what befits our expectations. Does adhering to a God who cannot compel do damage to the concept of what it means to be divine? This deity may leave fingerprints, but is ultimately handcuffed. Perhaps the more seasoned method would be to say that misfortunes occur, for the world is messy, and God remains God. Humans have been left to their own devices, for now. And the earth at times belches, twitches and hiccups, thereby generating natural disasters. At least this way one continues to live with the task of holding premises two and three in tension, along with the prospect that there are no easy solutions. No quick fixes, only tension. This leaves us with a complex God for a complex world.

Evolving

The final topic addresses the natural world, the third installment of which marks the transition to the second part of our study.

"Nature is red in tooth and claw." I used to think that Lord Tennyson overstated the case and in a sense still do. There is much harmony in the world where organisms occupy niches, or livelihoods, alongside others, often adopting a policy of laissez-faire economics with their neighbors. But this does not halt predator-prey relationships, nor does their interaction cease to be messy. On certain television documentaries on the animal kingdom, a snake is sometimes seen to dislocate its jaw, thereby enabling it to swallow its prey whole. These scenes often portray reptiles as adept at hunting, killing and devouring. Lizards tend to be particularly skilled in this. Perhaps my emphasis is reflective of an ancient revulsion toward our reptilian forebears who conveniently stepped aside allowing our more recent mammalian ancestors to succeed them. And good riddance!

When I observe predator-victors savoring the delicacies of their prey-victims, I cannot help but wonder if this can be an event over which the deity takes pleasure. I confess that I have difficulty believing that God would give this situation the divine seal of approval and exclaim, "Isn't this great?" Or is my visceral reaction one that the deity shares in? Consider three options. The first is analogous to an artist who finds satisfaction in his or her finished product, meaning God would still appraise this planet as very good as God allegedly did at the outset. If so, the offense I take is confined to myself and others who may think and feel likewise. Maybe God judges this as the cost of creating a skilled hunter through the evolutionary process. We, after all, are little different when we express our carnivorous side. We just do not often see the blood that gets spilled. We leave that up to the rendering plants, enabling us to ignore the fact that we, too, are killers. Even God in the account in Acts 10:9ff. tells Peter in his trance or vision to kill and eat the animals that God has provided for him. To fail to do so would be to reject a good gift on God's part. Could it be that this is the price to be paid for complex organisms requiring other complex organisms to replenish complex proteins? Vegetarianism and veganism are not in our nature. They must be learned.

I mentioned that there were three alternatives. Another is the notion that things were not always this way. Some might be inclined to point to a Golden Age in which there was no predator-prey relationship, or even death, and every organism was most likely a vegetarian (depending on whether cattle and chickens were domesticated and used for non-vegan purposes). There was harmony as far as the Garden extended. The spilling of blood became a consequence of God's curse and the expulsion from Eden. It is interesting to note, as outlined above, that God is the first one to have blood on the hands, for it was God who provided skins for the first human pair to wear subsequent to the recognition of their (then indecent) exposure. I find that I am disinclined to hold this position, not least of which is the reason that there appears to be no anthropological evidence for it, although it does explain the cursedness of our relation to the land and other life forms. It also gives me the impetus to act on the enmity between specific creatures and ourselves and wage war against them, especially those arachnids that dare to enter our abode.

A third possibility is that the world has evolved to a point where at least one creature can assess our current situation and evaluate it as deficient. It has been found wanting. There has to be a better way. The passage which the apostle Paul writes in Romans 8:22-3 is instructive here. The creation groans for the curse to be lifted. Groaning because it, too, laments the blood that falls upon it. The curse would then amount to the alienation that has been and continues to hold between and among creatures of all kinds in the biosphere. The creation awaits God's assistance in bringing this state of affairs to a close. Whereas the first approach understands the status quo in favorable terms, the third places it in an adverse light. I suggest that the third is the most likely candidate. At least it grants me the fortitude to stomach these documentaries.

Sustaining

Expanding on the above theme of diet, the Hippocratic-type of sentiment that intends to do no harm to others is well-intentioned; I can certainly appreciate that. But it is no less wide of the mark for being sincere. Regrettably, "no creatures were harmed in the making of this production" is an unattainable ideal. The mentality to "live and let live," an organismic "let it be," is commendable. Concern for the welfare of others is something we could all stand to aspire to. Yet, sadly, despite all our efforts, the system does not run this way; and biology makes all of us the culprits, whether we are conscious of it or not.

From the time that we are in the womb, we, by our very nature, are death-producing. At the fetus stage, there is a period when we have webbed feet (usually days 51-56). This is a natural occurrence, and most of us get over it. There are a few, however, who retain it. Webbing may perhaps be useful in our then aqueous confines, though we are not able to achieve much in the way of displacement. (Where precisely would we go?) But we are soon to lose this feature and that is known as cell death. Hence not all cell death is a negative thing. Furthermore, from our earliest moments, to keep us alive means the perishing of others—some of which formerly belonged to us. Every time we ingest, cells are scraped off our mouth, throat and intestinal walls. Our skin also loses a layer of cells periodically. Referred to as body ash, skin cells make the ultimate sacrifice in order to keep us alive, and this also accounts for much of the household dust that we encounter. So inside and out we lose cells on a continual basis. By killing parts of us, or at least letting them die, we remain a going concern.

Compounded with this is our immunological system, whose task it is to ward off microbiological offenders. It destroys them before they get an opportunity to destroy us. And all of this activity occurs as we go about our business, unaware that there is a battle raging. Moreover, we need to extend a concerted effort at hygiene to ensure that microbes do not get the better of us. Attending to personal maintenance is crucial so as not to be party to vectors of disease. (It appears our mothers were right.) We destroy so as to survive. Not all microbes are villainous, though. We also require them for self-preservation. Some are essential to our health and well-being, but only if they are in their proper places. Deviation can entail destruction, for which white-garbed professionals might need to be called in.

Beyond our personal selves, other aspects of the biosphere are also affected. For every square inch to which we lay claim is that much less that others can enjoy. To the extent that we have squatter's rights, or powers, others must squat elsewhere. Thus we are instrumental in the displacement of other creatures. Once we take our pick, there is less for others. The most desirable environment for us might mean the less desirable or even hostile for others. If we oust organisms from their environment, such as when a new residential subdivision is constructed, they need to retreat to ever-diminishing areas. This does not (although it can) ordinarily amount to a quick death for these displaced organisms, but perhaps a slow and painful one. Whether intended or not, the niche we occupy and the waste we generate threatens and hastens the extinction of other species (and ultimately our own). To expand our niche means to supplant the niche of others. This can lead to their extinction unless, through innovation, they are able to carve another.

Hence never mind a carnivorous diet: we are detrimental to other species simply by existing. At best, to live is to kill; at worst, to live is to make extinct. While this is not something about which humans need be vilified, for simply being human is not an indictable offense, it does raise awareness that we affect our surroundings, sometimes adversely. Optimally, consciousness of the consequences will lead to a conscience that would seek to minimize the harm. To attempt to survive is natural; to pursue a wider benefit is admirable.

Yet a previous question persists and begs reintroduction, namely, is God pleased to continue to manage God's economy this way? Or did it derail somewhere along the line?

Surviving

Organisms appear to be naturally conservative. They continue to do what they have done for a very long time, because it has worked for them. The status quo has a selective advantage, so long, that is, as circumstances remain the same. There might be a better way, but organisms tend to be pragmatic as well—if it works, why change? Should conditions become altered, however, conservatism gets shelved and organisms scramble liberally for cover, until such time as order, if ever for them, is restored.

It is easy to anthropomorphize and suggest that the behavior of organisms is analogous to that of humans. Female penguins, for instance, who lose a chick may try to steal one from a neighbor—the response toward which is outrage on the part of the group. They will seek to gang up on the perpetrator and halt the success of her quest and return the chick to its own mother. Can this reaction be considered a moral one, or are humans alone in this? Is ethics purely a human phenomenon? It might usually be understood as a stretch to draw ethical conclusions from animal behavior. Certain wasps have been known to lay eggs in caterpillars so that when the young hatch they have an immediate meal at hand. They eat the caterpillar from the inside and in the precise way so as to keep the victim alive as long as possible. This may strike us as horrific, but we are not the wasp (nor, I suspect would we care to be the caterpillar). Are these wasps to be judged as cruel? And what is the extent to which this reflects the divine economy or a cursed creation? Are only wasps granted the latitude that allows this as acceptable behavior?

Back to the example of the penguins, at the same time, oddly, they are not socialist in collective structure. For a chick that loses both its parents to death is abandoned, not embraced by the group. It might attempt to obtain food from a different or substitute mother, but it will be rejected. So much for displaying a conscience. It is curious that those mothers that lost their chicks, especially those that sought to steal a chick away from its rightful mother, are not united with those chicks that lost both parents. It seems that each would benefit from such an arrangement.

Perhaps God is of the conviction that it is better to have a chance at life than simply to avoid the hardships that go along with it and to forego the chance of vying for survival. In the interest of self-preservation, organisms could share this viewpoint. Our behavior seems to imply that the enduring of struggles is more than compensated for by projected lifespan; all the while recognizing, of course, that this prospect can be offset by the tragedy of the premature loss of a partner or offspring.

Maybe God is interested in maximizing the number of creatures that can simply experience God's cosmos—to heighten, that is, the "behold" factor. The trouble with this line of reasoning, though, is that there are those whose chance at life gets snuffed out in infancy, or worse, in the womb or egg, well before it might be cognizant of its surroundings. There would in such a case be no admirer of God's handiwork. Life may be a precious gift, but the natural world does not seem to cherish it.

"But we've never done it that way!" This is a common refrain expressed by certain conservative figures who have a vested interest in the maintenance of the status quo when confronted with a new idea or method of operation. Frustration levels can rise when innovators attempt to impress upon traditionalists that a new approach might be warranted, and also when keepers of the tried and true ask these promoters of the avant garde, "What was wrong with the old way of doing things?" Neither side appears to be effective in convincing the other to budge.

The tried and true also figures into the evolutionary scheme. There is a resistance to large-scale alterations for long periods of time in the fossil record. Stephen Jay Gould and Niles Eldredge have disclosed, though not without their detractors, that modifications in organisms amount to minor variations that do not necessarily lead to speciation. And when they do, they occur rapidly (at least in evolutionary timescales) and then remain in the new form for extended periods. The name given to this phenomenon is punctuated equilibria. New ways of doing things are seized upon, moreso than occurring by a gradual series of steps of accumulated variations over time.

What was once thought to be an oddity has become commonplace. Mainstream evolutionists may still hold to a gradualist regimen, while Gould (now deceased) and Eldredge embody the minority position. Yet anomalies seem to have a way of making their presence felt. The German physicist Max Planck was counseled by Lord Kelvin to avoid the field of physics as a career option, since there would be little left to accomplish in the discipline at his time (circa 1900). As soon as two anomalous phenomena— the photoelectric effect and black body radiation—submit to current accepted techniques (the conservative voice), physics would largely be done as a discipline. All that would remain is the technician's role of increasing the precision of measurements and calculations to additional decimal places. Planck, however, (the innovative voice) contended that what we have before us is not a task that requires mopping up but the basis for a new physics. Quantum mechanics, of which he was the main early representative, grew out of one of these anomalies and relativity theories out of the other. The previous Newtonian mechanistic view of the world then became not the rule but the exception. Two scientific revolutions were spawned by the work of Planck and Einstein. And we are the richer for it; the conservative approach would have left us impoverished.

The anomalies, though, do not end there. More recently it was uncovered that nonlinearity might be more ordinary than initially suspected. The cosmos was believed to run in a linear fashion with nonlinearity relegated to the periphery. Then along came Rene Thom and catastrophe theory, chaos and complexity theories, with terms like feedback and iteration, then Ilya Prigogine and dissipative structures, generating concepts such as order from systems far from equilibrium. Suddenly nonlinearity was cast into the limelight. So much so that now it is proposed that linearity might be the oddity in an otherwise nonlinear universe. The old radicalism has become the new conservativism.

Our horizons are broadened once we pay attention to the formerly marginalized or underappreciated. (As will be investigated below, this may also apply to images of the divine.) Lynn Margulis and Dorion Sagan (2002) have suggested that the main impetus or driving force behind natural selection is not the mutation-causing-variation idea that Charles Darwin looked for but never found. Darwin was unable to provide an explanation, that is, a mechanism, for the onset of variations in species. Much later it was "unearthed" that mutations caused by DNA recombination, radiation, chemical and other means account for these variations. The trouble remained, sadly, that mutations are vastly counterproductive. Nor is there overwhelming evidence that new species necessarily arise strictly on the basis of these mutations. Margulis and Sagan propose that an alternate perspective is called for. Once again, this concerns the anomalous.

They draw support for their view from the microbiological world. The plants known as lichens, which are combinations of fungi and algae, are perhaps the prime example of an association of two different types of organisms. This communal aspect of evolution is referred to as symbiosis, where multiple organisms benefit from an intimate arrangement. In this case, fungi and algae cooperate to produce a thriving organism where alone they might not survive. Adaptation here means an integration of entire genomes—an organism's genetic complement. Margulis and Sagan perceive this approach as explaining what Darwin and his successors still cannot. For these two researchers, integration occurs at four increasing levels of intimacy: behavioral, metabolic, gene-product and genetic (Margulis & Sagan, 101). Whereas it was suspected that evolution always operates by way of species divergence, integration of entire genomes is a case of convergence. And apparently this anomalous situation is much more prevalent than first conceded.

Will this lead to a revolution similar in scale to those heralded by Planck, Einstein and others? Maybe not. But is this another instance where the marginal may become the norm? Margulis and Sagan believe so. As the search continues for other phenomena which are ordinarily interpreted as anomalous, how many more "demarginalizations" can we expect?

This leads us into the second part of our study.

PART TWO

The Nature of the Natural

Just a Curiosity at Best?

PART ONE LEAVES US WITH A QUESTION, namely, is the divinity depicted in the Judeo-Christian scriptures an accurate reflection of what was experienced? Does the reporting lose something in the translation from witness to portrayal? There are those among us who would respond with a resounding affirmative to the second question and a negative to the first.

As we begin a new section, I want to start with a perplexing question—at least one that, for me, confounds resolution, but perhaps not progress. I have often wondered what would behoove a divinity to leave us in this world to fend for ourselves in a way that resembles abandonment. I perceive far too many hazards in living in the world that could really stand some divine assistance. And to top it all off, life is not very efficient either, since much of our time is devoted to sleep, attending to personal maintenance, chores, errands and, heaven forbid, repairs. The stock answers on the part of classical theists are either that God in fact *is* present through the Spirit and/or that God does not stick around where God is not wanted. Having already addressed the former, here is a comment on the latter. We are on our own because, in effect, we have asked God to leave us alone. We have given God the cold shoulder. While it is tempting to think in these terms, the classical God seems to exercise its muscles more. This God does not appear to take no for an answer, but rolls up its sleeves and is ready to do battle. In part three we will discuss various portraits of divinity against the philosophical and theological systems that gave rise to them. In the meantime, let's take a walk on the following path.

The Genesis account of the creation of humans and their downfall may be mythical, but it also might contain a germ of truth about the human condition. Would life in the Garden have had comparable hazards and pitfalls as we experience here? Was there a danger that gravity would have let fly with, say, a coconut (for the Garden was said to have contained "all kinds of trees" [Genesis 2:9, NIV]) which could have landed on the head of Adam? If so, then God had a laissez-faire policy even prior to the fall of humans. If not, then God was pleased to intervene. Unless, of course, there are other options. If these circumstances prevailed subsequent to God's curse on humans and creation, we could put it down to life in a distorted world, much like the question asked in the previous paragraph. But if they also occurred prior to the time of the fall and the curse, could they have been avoided through faculties that God imparted to humans but have since been lost? Call them, perhaps, powers of anticipation. Recall I mentioned that the accounts are mythical, but may the authors have captured something currently unrecognized about early humans contained in some type of collective unconscious? Even the use of a term such as this suggests that our forebears might have been able to tap in to an ability or awareness that neither registers to us today nor no longer impresses us to nurture it. Was there in fact an ancestral capacity that twenty-first century sensibilities would evaluate as pseudo-scientific, not worthy of mention? For some, it is a question of credibility, and these anomalies, if they are real, do not contain enough of it. This is one thing that I wish to pursue here.

On a topic to be enlarged upon in Part Three, the attributes of God can be subdivided into two categories, specifically metaphysical and moral, where humans can participate in the latter but not the former. I mention this because it is pertinent for the theme of the image of God. Humans are allegedly created in this *imago Dei*, but it takes some effort to disclose in what it might consist, for that is not straightforward. When we attempt to delineate what separates humans from the other animals—note our kinship with creatures—the differences are not altogether obvious. This stands to reason, since all living things can be traced back to a common ancestor. Each species bears a different complement of DNA, but the genetic material is the same. We all derived from an early living form, though not necessarily the first, since this might not have been the successful one to pass on its genes to subsequent generations. The initial trial may have been a failure.

Most of the capacities that humans enjoy can also be found elsewhere in the animal kingdom. Other organisms use tools (some birds, for example); still others communicate through the use of symbols—or at least can be taught to do so (some birds, some primates, and social insects, such as the dances of bees) and some even plan for an albeit limited future (the food storage habits of squirrels). Though if we are pressed, we can indeed point to a number of activities we perform which bear no analog or counterpart in the biosphere, such as the preparation and paying of taxes, or the use of currency for trade, which itself otherwise has no objective value (unless in the absence of a proper tool, dimes, say, can be used to turn screws). Perhaps, although this might be a stretch, no other creature also worries. Prey can constantly be on the alert about the presence of predators and in a moment's notice, the time it takes for adrenalin to deliver its rush, is ready for fight or flight. But this is not the same as worry. Maybe our five- and ten-year plans as well as retirement aspirations bring with them anxiety about what the future may hold. Other creatures appear to be preoccupied solely with the mindset some have counselled humans to adopt, namely living for the present moment. Only humans have medicine cabinets filled with pharmaceuticals, and perhaps even non-prescription substances, geared "to take the edge off."

The Bible offers some indication as to what it means to be human. Taking the text at face value for a moment, the best clues we obtain involve what humans were like before the alleged Fall from grace through disobedience, for after this event both humans and the rest of creation became distorted. Prior to the Fall, humans were intended to be moral creatures—something which carries over into the post-Fall era—and so perhaps this implies that to bear the image means to participate in God's moral attributes. Yet this cannot be all there is to it. We apparently also enjoy free will in addition to creativity, some of which is manifested in our tasks. Mention has already been made of the original task of tending to the Garden. Subsequent to the curse, however, humans are also asked to have faith and hope in the divinity, with charity understood as a divine attribute which we have also been called to express. But there is still more—I suspect a good deal more, though the image should at least amount to this. Consider that in Genesis 2:19-20, God brings before Adam all the animals God has made (note no plants) allowing the first human to give names to them, much like a child gets to name the family pet. (Part of the exercise, I suppose, was to demonstrate to this biblical character that no other creature is human, for no partner for Adam could be found from among them.) This makes humans taxonomists. Humans engage in ordering, systematizing and classifying things into categories and naming them. We tend to look for patterns.

A classification scheme is what I want to focus on, for along with it come assumptions about the nature of the creatures that bear a certain name—what they must be like and how they must behave. Placing a grid on something means that it must conform to expectations. Otherwise the world would not seem orderly. And if it is not, then our scheme needs adjustment, for the world does not always function according to our notions of it and will not adjust to our ideas. Here is my concern: the fit or potential gap between our description of the world and its actual operation. Naturally, our descriptions are only ever approximations of the way the world works, but about this we seem to require constant reminding. For the tendency is to lapse into a false sense of security that the territory and our map of it are one and the same, which Alfred North Whitehead refers to as the fallacy of misplaced concreteness—mistaking the abstract for the concrete. The topics broached here in this introduction as well as some of those alluded to in Part One will be elucidated in what follows. So let us observe some of the ways in which Lyall Watson describes the world.

(This now takes the form of a timely tribute, as Watson "crossed over" at the age of 69 on June 25, 2008, as the first draft of the present work came to completion.)

Extraordinary Life

Lyall Watson earned a doctorate in animal behavior under Desmond Morris at the London Zoo and has worked as an anthropologist, archaeologist, paleontologist, marine biologist, botanist and medical researcher. His interests and abilities are extensive. Taking our cues from his studies, let us ascend the evolutionary scale of complexity, beginning with "ordinary" organic matter.

The first item of note is the range of living forms and their habitats. Organisms are widespread, at least on our planet, but they are contained within a very narrow range of a different sort. The electromagnetic scale of radiation extends through an enormous range of frequencies and wavelengths, but only a minuscule amount of it amounts to visible light. All of life as we know it is restricted to this narrow bandwidth. Life cannot survive for long in ultraviolet light (wavelengths shorter than visible light) and beyond, nor in infrared (longer) and beyond. Our sun shines ultravioletly but also in this visible range, specifically in the yellow portion of the spectrum. Thankfully, much of its ultraviolet rays are absorbed by a layer of ozone in our atmosphere (though it has experienced trying times recently). And gratefully, life flourishes in the range in which the sun shines. Further, "the amount of energy contained in visible light is perfectly matched to the energy needed to carry out most chemical reactions" (1974a, 16). Lucky for us and the rest of life.

Yet our corner of the universe is not the only place where organic material is located. The entire amount by weight of organic matter (those carbon-based chemical compounds found in life forms) to inorganic for our planet is a meager one ten-millionth of one percent. In contrast, of all the material which is transported to earth from outer space, one tenth of one percent is organic. This is a staggering difference, for it implies that these extraterrestrial packages, often in the form of meteors, for instance, "are coming from somewhere that is [or was] a million times more organic than the earth itself" (1980, 33). Our self-imposed uniqueness has taken a hit.

The first stop on the evolutionary tour of life are single- and multi-cellular microorganisms. For our purposes, though, we will skip ahead and concentrate on the already more complex and potentially macroscopic plants or animals known as parasites. These creatures are characteristically "all take and no give." They rob from other organisms and offer nothing in return. But as Watson points out, "Killing your host is bad for business" (1980, 43). It does not help your own cause, for once your host is dead, you are out of luck and viable accommodations. For this reason, both host and intruder have over the ages developed an arrangement in which both benefit to some extent. This more adaptive mutual approach is known as symbiosis and it assists in making the business of life a going concern. The continued survival of both is good for business.

This implies that parasites are "still in an early stage of adaptation" in evolutionary history and "must be new to the job" (1980, 44). You can tell if it's a new kid on the block when it hasn't yet learned to bend a little. Parasites, however, come in various shapes and sizes. We could also be considered as "parasites on the skin of our planet." Our success depends not only on learning to "become aware of its pulse and ... to pace our lives to [its] rhythm" (1974a, 21), but also to contribute to the earth's well-being in true symbiotic fashion. The planet is our host and we ought to be good guests or tenants.

Skill in adaptation can further be observed in plants. Some are adept at responding to the insects that come to visit. As Watson uncovers, "flying insects become highly charged in flight as a result of their rapid wingbeats. And it appears that [the plant] *Biophytum* has learned to react to the presence of such an electrostatic field in the air by taking appropriate avoiding action [by letting its leaflets droop] even before an approaching insect has a chance to land." This has ramifications for us as well. As Watson continues, "the possibility of reaction to, and interaction with, the fields produced by some humans no longer seems quite so outrageous. Perhaps those of us who seem to have "green fingers and thumbs" are simply better earthed [or grounded] than others, giving off none of the negative action potentials that stimulate some plants into taking evasive action, and remind others of traumas produced by old wounds and injuries" (1986, 44-45).

The astounding adaptations do not end there. Certain North American trees respond to insect offenders by producing chemicals noxious to them. A similar reaction occurs in the African savannah where certain trees prevent creatures like giraffes from overindulging on them. The truly remarkable thing in both cases is that neighboring untouched trees are reported as showing the same response. Researchers suspect that the assaulted plants "must be releasing pheromones, airborne hormones that are carried on the wind like alarm-calls, warning trees in [the vicinity] of the danger of imminent attack by insect [and other] predators, and leading them to make their own preparations to meet the onslaught" (1986, 46). These are some of the botanical defense mechanisms and "pre-emptive precautions" observed in action. An indication that plants can also have their higher organismic moments, despite not possessing a central nervous system, is that they too can be anaesthetized. Ether and chloroform have similar effects on plants as on organisms with a brain. I suppose it is reasonable to assume that since many natural pharmaceuticals come from plants, such as ASA (aspirin), that they should have a beneficial effect on them as well (1986, 46-47).

If plants have capacities for which we do not ordinarily give them credit, then does the same hold true for animals? Watson detects, for instance, that the known sensitivity of oysters to lunar effects on tides can extend to circumstances in which they have been relocated inland. They can adjust to such an upheaval and "[open] up at the time the tide would have flooded" the new location. And what is more, the phenomenon occurs even if they are kept in the dark away from the cues of sunrise and sunset. Watson announces that "This was the first piece of scientific evidence to show that even an organism living away from the ocean tides could be influenced by the passage of the moon" and adjust its timetable accordingly. A possible conclusion to be drawn from this account is that if lunar gravity affects a large body of water, it can also act on the small. The major constituent of organisms, after all, is water, which can be altered in non-negligible ways by a competing gravitational force. One laboratory has even developed equipment "so sensitive that it has been able to record lunar tides in a cup of tea" (1974a, 23-24). It appears that organisms also possess such sensitivity, whether they are attuned to it or not.

Another startling animal capability is seen in the monarch butterfly. As snowbirds retreat to warmer climes in order to escape northern winters, so monarchs have long adopted similar vacation plans. They migrate to "Mexico and return along the same routes the following spring." They travel "over 100 kilometres a day, stopping each night to rest in ... particular trees—the same [ones] every year." Both we and they can be creatures of habit, though monarchs carry it to an extreme. They persistently manage to "pick out the traditional motel trees, despite the fact that the [ones flying] in any year are first- or even second-generation offspring of those that covered the course in the opposite direction the previous season" (1986, 66). I realize the need to make travel plans well ahead of time, and I have also heard of people bequeathing season's tickets to sporting events in wills to next of kin, but this seems to combine the two. Somehow the butterflies yet to be born receive the memo for future excursions, many of which only ever experience one stage of it. Perhaps space travel will require humans to subscribe to a similar strategy.

Before we proceed to human considerations, I present the following digression.

History is written by the victors. No argument there, though it needs to be appreciated that this can extend even into the scientific arena. The history of science is not currently written by proponents of aether or phlogiston theories, unless it is by way of apology. There was a time when these views were counted among the ranks of conventional wisdom. To detract from them in their heyday would have been met with derision. Then when the tide turned, those who scoffed initially might have joined the chorus in scoffing the now superseded view. They may chime in with, "How could we have ever thought that way?" (although the Flat-Earth Society continues to boast members).

When we write our own history from an evolutionary standpoint, it betrays a "fitter-than-thou" attitude. And if we are even less careful, this could deteriorate into an anthropocentric one. To "we are the champions" can be added "and we were destined to be." But if approached more accurately, reasons that species survive can be more precarious than genotype and phenotype, for at times it can hang on quirks of history. I do not intend to suggest that biological accounts are flawed, though they might be just that, but that biology is incomplete without history. Individual survival may hang in the balance of extra-biological factors. The dinosaurs found this out, albeit their reign had already peaked and they could have been in for a steady decline, becoming too big for their own good, too much time devoted just for sustenance of their large frames. The extraterrestrial object only hastened their demise.

In addition to a genetic account, a falling tree here and a rockslide there, neither functioning with malice aforethought, can also alter the course of evolutionary history. Admittedly, theorists do recognize chance as part of the proceedings, yet this is often in the form of adaptive variations or changes in climatic conditions. I am instead referring to the hazards of living. At a certain point in prehistory, a promising individual with a beneficial variation, hard to come by as they are, might have been felled by a falling branch. Through no biological fault of its own, it was in the wrong place at the wrong time. There is no gene for avoiding it. And the description of the event is an historical component of an overall biological explanation. There are biological reasons why some creatures are spared from mass extinctions; there are historical reasons why the dinosaurs died before their time. Both are operative in evolution. Both history and biology happen to organisms.

The Personal Touch

I want to begin discussing human life by referring to death. Death is a part of life and does not always occur at its conclusion. There is a good deal of us that is dead, even now. We are covered with it. I speak of, among other things, our epidermal layer. Our outer skin cells are dead. When looking at someone, "There is not a living cell in sight." "Life [not] only depends on death" but "relies on [an optimal] combination of both." In Watson's words, "We owe our lives not only to the cells that erect a barrier between us and the outside world," one purpose of which is to keep us safe from exposure to the ravages of oxygen, "but also to armies of others that regularly lay down their lives in internal battles dedicated to" our longevity, by which he means our white blood cells. We have a constant turnover of cells at different rates, depending on the organ in question. This connotes that "Death is programmed into life," thereby ensuring our survival, provided that "death of certain of [our] parts occurs on schedule" (1974b, 24-25).

A thorny philosophical issue emerges from the foregoing, namely, what makes us who we are? If we encounter a seven-year cycle of physical renewal, where by the end of that time nearly every molecule in our body has been recycled, then what is it about us that endures? Is there a continuity of personhood? Toward offering a solution, Watson contributes the following:

> We carry a reminder of who we are in every blood cell. A sense of identity is basic to all life, even at the cellular level. It is responsible for all immune and allergic reactions, for the way in which white blood cells reject and remember foreign bodies, producing specific antibodies in anticipation of future invasions. And it is the secret of successful cohesion between all the millions of cells which form part of the same body. Our health depends on it. Otherwise [our organs] would all have their own agendas and tend to pull in opposite directions. (1995, 43)

Old blood cells are also flushed out of our system and created anew in bone marrow, each new supply coming with a recognition of who "us" is and who "them" are. "Us" becomes protected, while "them" are opposed. It's nice to be remembered. (It is also fortunate and advantageous that a foreign body response of our immunological system toward an intruder is not usually elicited against an embryo or fetus in the gestation period, except in the case of miscarriages.)

On the topic of friend or foe, our nature appears to bear direct responsibility for classifying the world according to a dichotomy of "members versus non-members." Watson calls this "one of the few true human universals." People have a history of dividing the world along group or even tribal lines. This can have disastrous consequences, not least of which is the danger of viewing outsiders as subhuman—a different species (1995, 127-28). But we no longer need to go to these lengths to ensure survival value. Evidently, not everything that is detrimental gets weeded out.

If *Homo sapiens* as a species were to draft a curriculum vitae, first among the items in the experience section would be hunter-gatherers for a very long stretch of time. We have a lengthy track record of having "learned to become practicing, habitual carnivores." In this we differ from most other primates, as well as, of course, on the issue of body hair. There are occasions, however, when "several primates, particularly baboons and chimpanzees, when they can, will kill and eat small [game]" (1983, 32). What is learned, though, could become unlearned or even re-educated after a period of time. Earlier in the biblical section, I mentioned that vegetarianism and veganism need to be learned. More precisely, they have already been unlearned in our distant past when we took on a carnivorous (or omnivorous—we have not lost our taste for bananas, for example) lifestyle. This has had a head start on the order of one million years and is not likely to be readily undone.

Watson applies this line of thinking to a related topic:

> Any strategy that lasts for several million years is worth taking seriously. It has earned its evolutionary spurs, done what it takes to be described as a success in Darwinian terms. While "civilisation," the lifestyle that we have been experimenting with [for many thousands of years]—just [a small percentage] of our time in the arena— has to be described as an interesting, troubled and still unproven solution (1995, 143).

Culture is also not something we would seek to do without any time soon. And it adds another component to the evolutionary calculations. Prior to culture, the genes ruled and we were subject to their oppressive regime. We now enjoy the wherewithal to give genes themselves some competition—a run for their organismic money. We have stumbled upon cultural evolution "which, compared to the biological process, happens at the speed of light" (1995, 209). Genetic evolution, being biochemical, is Darwinian/Mendelian and tardy; cultural evolution is Lamarckian and hasty. Both have their benefits and drawbacks (how, for instance, did we ever survive disco?). Culture can be passed on quickly through education. Genetics must simmer. Also, "Natural selection is extraordinarily good at maximizing immediate genetic interests, but it is uncommonly bad at long-term planning." Culture can be transmitted via social contact with other members of our species. Consequently, "We have, to a very large extent, liberated ourselves from strict genetic control and put a rival pattern of inheritance in play" (1995, 238).

We are still attempting to delineate here in our study the uniqueness of humans. The fact that we are having difficulty is testimony to the notion that we have an evolutionary lineage. It should therefore not strike us as odd that there is continuity with other species. To belong to this biological tradition means that "Not one of our abilities can be denied to some other animal somewhere, but what we have done is to arrange everything in an entirely new way." For Watson, no appeal to an outside source need be made: "none of [our] qualities is new. No component of our brain or behavior has been added by supernatural means to make us what we are" (1974a, 184). Yet only humans engage in culture, despite the reference to the care of bees as apiculture. Social insects, like ants, bees, termites and wasps, interact for a common goal, sometimes with the suggestion that the group constitutes one organism, but division of labor by itself does not a culture make. Albeit for them it is not haphazard—there are appreciable results of their toil. And while culture can be "inherited or replicated," neither form of evolution can account for the generation of a new idea (1995, 237). Innovation can be found across the species barrier—birds in their history have found novel uses for their beaks, such as searching for food in the bark of trees when supplies are low, for instance. Once again, humans are not alone in such endeavors. Other species can also be resourceful in obtaining resources.

Let us now return to a noticeable difference.

I have a few comments on the following excerpt of Watson which deals with the above themes, and for this we will need to reproduce it in its entirety (it bears repeating at length anyway).

> The one weapon that is unquestionably ours is human speech, and the fossils it leaves in the form of the written or printed word. With these, we have a system of information transmission which is a real rival to genetic reproduction. Cultural evolution is very much like genetic evolution in that progress can be tracked by the effects each has on individuals who receive them. Memes [the fundamental units of cultural inheritance] rise and fall in a population exactly as genes do, spreading in an environment that is favourable to them, slipping into extinction where they fail to find such favour. New ideas, new music, new foods, new fashions and new faiths all succeed or fail on their merits. The difference is that, unlike the genes, they do not necessarily have to contribute to fitness in any way. Celibacy, hard rock, sushi, nipple rings and walking over hot coals have no obvious survival value, except as stimuli that can keep big brains busy and amused. At least for a while. They are not subject to natural selection, but are liable to be lost as soon as they fail to satisfy an equally natural human curiosity.(1995, 240)

To begin with, speech is not unique to us, for other species communicate through sounds, such as the songs of whales. So the word "and" in the first sentence should be replaced with "though only in the case of." Next, as far as I can determine, Watson contradicts himself when he claims that on the one hand cultural evolution is analogous to Darwinian/Mendelian inheritance in that memes—products of culture—are similar to genes, and on the other that they are not subject to natural selection. Genetic evolution is all about natural selection; so to declare, if I understand him correctly, that memes are analogous to genes is undermined if natural selection does not apply to culture. If he wishes to make the case that cultural products are in fact free from issues of fitness, then no such analogy can be drawn.

Finally, having said this, and contrary to Watson, cultural products can actually be the objects on which natural selection operates. Culture produces pharmaceuticals, life jackets, bullet-proof cars and so on, all of which clearly have survival value. Hence the case could be made that culture sounds genetic if natural selection applies. A bullet-proof vest has survival value for a law-enforcement official whose longevity is enhanced and who can then be the recipient of scarce natural resources and provide for a mate so as to live long enough to pass genes on to the next generation. This measures success rate, and that is natural selection. Thus cultural evolution can play into genetic evolution. Culture can instruct individuals so that they are more survival savvy. The information learned in boy scouts, for instance, can assist in self-preservation skills. Natural selection acts on those who fend for themselves in the woods. Recalling important directions taught in scout camp have natural selection effects. In my estimation, Watson does not fully appreciate the similarity.

A question that can be posed is, can natural selection be combatted and is it ever appropriate to do so? One approach to take is in the field of medicine. Medical science is in the business of lengthening the quantity and heightening the quality of life. Where some patients struggle with heart conditions, insert pacemakers or carry out the procedure of bypass surgery. Where there is diabetes, plug insulin into the equation. Whereas these traits, and many others, would be acted upon by natural selection, medicine steps in to forestall and perhaps even reverse the severity. Cultural evolution affects genetic evolution. It allows weak genes to prosper and even proliferate in the population, against natural selection. Yet is it proper to work in opposition to it? Ask a diabetic. For folks such as these, natural selection needs to be fought against.

But another tack can be taken. Is there anything that humans do that is not natural? Some might insist that it is not natural to interfere with natural selection, though what could be more natural than self-preservation? Harmful variations get weeded out in evolution. Interfering with natural selection extends the life of the unfit. Yet as products of natural selection, is everything we do natural? We do not cease to be subject to it despite medical science. Natural selection got us here. Is this how we show our gratitude? A possible response is that in spite of being products of the evolutionary process, we can now move beyond it. Nature is now in a position to work against itself. Natural selection has yielded organisms that can militate against it. This becomes advantageous, adaptive and increases fitness and survival value. One way of viewing the situation is that in this respect natural selection has worked itself out of a job; and in another, natural selection has produced not a human answer to it but a different version of it. Human nature is combatting nature and winning this round. (Beware the tendency to separate humans from nature, for humans *are* natural and a part of nature.) This battle goes to humans, but not the war. Ultimately, humans will go the way of all species. They will have, on the average, five million years of fame (or what in evolutionary historical terms very much amounts to fifteen minutes) and will then see their demise. The effects of natural selection can be curbed or restrained but not halted. It can afford to be patient.

Back to the question of human nature, perhaps what makes us human is the interest in devising and observing codes of conduct. We are moral creatures. That is, our actions have an ethical component, whether we elect to adhere to moral conventions or not. We evaluate the behavior of others according to some standard and are ourselves measured against often the same or similar one. The categories of stimulus and response do not adequately describe why we do what we do. Faith, hope and charity take on an added dimension. In the vast majority of cultures, there does appear to be "an implicit understanding that we ought to be able by now to do better than the genetic minimum. Human nature is no longer inevitable ... Thus 'Nature, [according to some], is what we are put in this world to rise above'" (1995, 248).

Here are some comments. First, I suspect that non-supernaturalists would care to substitute terms like "we *find* ourselves in this world" for our having been "put" or "placed here." On the other side, non-traditional theists could be prompted to object that if nature is so odious, then why did God, in God's wisdom, see fit to introduce us, through whatever means, into it as part of it? And incidentally, the idea of this genetic minimum is another factor, for me at least, which indicates that we bear in our makeup a biological instead of a specially created past. The unsavory aspects of our nature that we need to overcome are not as a result of an historical Fall, but a lengthy evolutionary process. The issue is not original sin but sustained genetic predispositions. What sustained us in the past has now become harmful to ourselves and others as culture itself has evolved.

In all fairness, certain genetic imperatives can and should be superseded. The trouble is, not only do we fail always to live up to them, we sometimes use our faculties in the service of even more egregious and erroneous ways. Commenting on the injustices in Rwanda of some time ago, Watson bemoans that "This is Armageddon with commercial breaks, evidence that the demons are not just among us—they are us" (1995, 132, 251). Better maybe to concentrate on our similarities rather than our differences, a consideration to be extended to the entire biosphere. Having the same common ancestor, all life is united. There is wisdom in the notion that the world of living things is a web of interconnections. Watson concludes that our commonality with other organisms constitutes "ties that bind all life together and that [humans], for all [their] special features, [are] an integral part of this whole" (1974a, 42).

In the Eye of the Beholder

Some people are keenly interested in patterns. This is what keeps criminologists and novelists, among others, employed. (It also indicates why *Wheel of Fortune* has had a longstanding audience.) Patterns need not be of human origin for them to have an impact on humans. Nature on its own also expresses them; the world is replete with cycles and rhythms. Watson discloses that "Life keeps time, and it seems that the beat is an old one, determined mainly by the rotation of our planet, which turns the sun on and off like some giant cosmic strobe light" (1974a, 16). While this example may be obvious, others are not so conspicuous. Our ability to hear is in the range of 20 to 20,000 Hertz (Hz) or cycles per second. Whereas sounds emanating outside of this range do not impact us, we may not be entirely oblivious to them. Our insensitivity does not entail a complete unawareness.

In Watson's view, "earthquakes make our whole planet ring like a gong, setting up long-wave, low-frequency oscillations that go on for an hour or more and can be measured anywhere on earth. These vibrations [fall into the alpha range and] occur at frequencies from seven to fourteen [Hz], and the fascinating thing about them is that they not only accompany, but also precede the actual occurrence of a quake. They provide an early warning system" (1989, 80). Notably, several species recognize these signals and respond to them (1974a, 94). Watson believes that our inundation in the electromagnetic fields of our own making—another type of pollution, though a more insidious one in that it affects everyone and, on the earth's surface at least, cannot be escaped—clouds the receptors that we once enjoyed. With them we were cognizant of the pulse and rumblings of our planet and were better able to diagnose the "signs of the times." Given our current bombardment, however, these voices are muted (1989, 83). Watson even goes so far as to exclaim that all organisms come with a capacity for awareness, whether of these rhythms or otherwise (1987, 68).

If even lower life forms enjoy awareness—bacteria know enough to recoil from an adverse pH gradient as we would pull a finger away from a hot element—then not only should ours be far superior given our relative complexity, but could we also cultivate (or rekindle) a heightened sense of our own? Does some amount lie dormant after ages of disuse? Have we become negligent and flabby in this regard? A few words are in order about our powers of observation.

The Western world likes to make distinctions. Aristotle's insight inspired the belief that making them is instrumental in leading toward knowledge. Confusion can be sorted out once a distinction is made, and slotting into categories spells relief and yields understanding. To make sense of the world requires an exercise of sorting and means that a grid is placed upon it. In the interest of mental control we insist that the world conform to our picture of it. This implies that we come with expectations about the world and it makes for uneasiness when the unexpected surfaces. Our reactions to surprises tell us more about us than the rest of the world. Watson diagnoses the malady this way: "Our Western system of intelligence began by dividing the world into equally fragmentary facts and events. It stressed the integrity of objects and the independence of ideas. It set things apart from one another" (1976, 192). There are a host of difficulties with such a naive concept.

The first problem Watson uncovers is with the methodology of objectification. For instance, we have a different view of the saliva in our mouths when we mix it with our meals versus if it were first to be deposited in a glass of our favorite beverage. This well known example illustrates the distance which the scientific approach places between subject and object, observer and observed. Science seeks to examine, for observation is a path to knowledge, but knowing our saliva better through laboratory tests does not make us any more willing to swallow it if it is initially separated from us. This is because "Detachment and perspective do permit pattern recognition, but they also produce alienation." Once external to me, saliva becomes a foreign object. Consequently, "a wedge has been driven between us. And I am wary of that wedge because it makes an observer of me when I feel that we should now be more concerned with our roles as participants" (1986, 20-21).

A second consideration is the limitations of our sensory capacities. We rely on our senses for observation, but they function adequately only within a certain range. Scientists may judge that there are apparati for much of the remainder, but even that remains restricted—confined to an albeit wider range. Equipment of any kind, biological or electronic, will ultimately be limited. We do not know what, if anything, lies beyond cosmic rays at one end of the electromagnetic spectrum or beyond radio waves at the other. Nor are we privy to what lies beyond the horizon of our visible universe, if the laws and forces there are the same as here and if its constituent particles are matter or antimatter. All sciences and all disciplines for that matter offer us merely a partial picture of reality. We all come with blinders that we cannot remove. Watson puts it in these terms: "Human vision responds to wavelengths from 380 to 760 millimicrons, which is exactly the range of frequencies least affected by the protective blanket of the atmosphere. We get a selective picture of the cosmos through a number of narrow windows of this kind in our sensory system" (1974a, 78).

Watson refers to "All sensation as biased," which then "becomes further distorted" when the brain gets through with it. Far from the objectivity which is one goal of scientific methodology, subjectivity cannot be avoided. The brain's contribution is to shuffle the sensory cues it receives into a workable portrait of them. But they must first get past the censor. We ultimately sense what we expect or are accustomed or are trained to sense. Such selectivity produces a gap between reality and our perception of it. Watson calls this the "censorship of the senses" on the part of the brain, where "Sensation [becomes] an abstraction, not a replication of reality" (1989, 62-63).

To make matters worse, "Our window on the world is already restricted by the reducing valve of our senses, and it gets even further circumscribed by language" (1987, 245). Our efforts to describe what we sense, filtered as it is through our neuronal network, leaves us at an additional remove from pure observation and objectivity. This is precisely the point made in the second question with which Part Two commenced. Yet Watson declares that we can take heart, for "We have an inherent and childlike talent for synaesthesia, for putting things together in new and unexpected ways, creating bypasses round the[se] reducing valves" (1989, 64). There might be something ostensibly unique about us after all.

There seems to be a three-step approach to perception. The first, according to Watson, is that "Our senses mould and shape information to suit their own ends;" the second concerns the brain as reorganizing its input "until they fall into some acceptable pattern;" and as for the third, "Reason is imposed on reality and alters it almost at will." The result is an advancing spiral of theory affecting observation, which in turn influences theory, and so forth. This precludes all potential for objectivity. "Our grasp of reality,... has been processed through the mill of our needs and our beliefs." And the statement "I wouldn't have believed it, if I hadn't seen it" can become "I wouldn't have seen it at all, if I hadn't already believed it in the first place" (1980, 249-50, 283). This has disturbing implications for both science and religion, as does the following.

The classical Newtonian paradigm of a mechanistic universe "reduced the world to building blocks." The new view of physics imagines the world as in a process of becoming. To Watson's thinking, "If *reality* flows like a stream, then *knowledge* of [it] also becomes fluid, a process rather than a set of fixed truths" (1987, 275). When one encounters experiences described as out-of-the-ordinary, the observers likely become perplexed because of our presuppositions about reality. We assume that perception "is a facsimile of what is being perceived, and that memory provides a facsimile of an original experience. Nothing could be further from the truth" (1980, 251) (supposing, of course, that there is in fact a *bona fide* non-theory-laden, non-agenda-driven truth to speak of).

Sometimes attaching a name to an object is one way of controlling part of our environment. In the ancient world, and as in the story of Adam who was given the task of naming all the animals, to know the name of someone or something is to have power over it. There is another human inclination here: "in practice our actual [sensory] sensitivity tends to be limited to the [stimulus] we can put a name to. People in different cultures even seem to divide the visible spectrum up [sic] differently, actually seeing a rainbow each in their own peculiar way ... It isn't easy to experience the unnamed, the unfamiliar. And the things we have named, tend to take on the characteristics we expect of them" (1980, 282). Quoting an additional source, Watson uncovers another human propensity: "names are far more than convenient labels or useful social decals. Words actually structure and reorganize reality, making it part of our experience. Naming ... gives each thing a 'handle' and a status quite independent of its function. I suggest that we may well be making the world up as we go along. Did all those subatomic particles exist before the physicists set out to look for them?" (1991, 43). If we had not looked, would we have missed them or would they have failed to materialize? Does our observing them manifest them?

Inroads for the Divine?

As Michael Polanyi pointed out and as Watson echoes, knowledge derived from perception is not passive but actively personal. Humans are involved in what they know—they take an active role in organizing and shaping their knowledge. This makes the purity of knowing forever beyond our grasp. Watson then employs this for a decidedly different turn. In his unguarded metaphysical moments, he announces that, given the powers of the human sensory apparatus outlined above, teamed up as they are with the central nervous system—a fine conspiracy theory—he envisions no reason "to posit unearthly elements in order to account for what seem to be supernatural events" (1980, 312). We alluded to this before, and here we elaborate on it. The notion of a beyond is thus explained for Watson as a product of human imagination and creativity. For him, the world is supernatural enough. No need, then, in true parsimonious fashion, to postulate anything more than material reality.

An example of his confidence in this idea follows. In his view, "A very weak electrical or magnetic field becomes noticeable because it resonates on the same frequency as the life field of the organism reacting to it. In this way, subtle stimuli, too small to make any impression on the normal senses, are magnified and brought to our notice. The supernatural becomes part of natural history" (1974a, 96).

At least two approaches are open to us here. We may conclude that this might well be how the divinity operates, employing an aspect of the world already at its disposal so as to convey some, albeit subtle, information. Or we could dismiss it and other instances like it as nothing more than the world at work, thereby explaining the supernatural away. For Watson, biology is sufficiently broad to encompass all counterintuitive occurrences. He also invites us to consider an example closer to home: "we are more likely, in the presence of incense, to experience the sort of communal ecstatic feelings on which organized religion depends for success. If there is a 'God gene,' which predisposes us to accept the idea of a deity, it may be sparked into action by the kind of basic biological euphoria that incense stirs in us" (2000, 154). In his appraisal, chemistry can affect biology in ways that would otherwise be interpreted as religious experience. But for Watson, we need not venture that far.

Recalling a previous theme, to be human means to bear "an innate drive to transcend." Watson mentions the case of "children in every culture [who] love to whirl like dervishes until they experience vertigo and collapse." While this is not strictly indicative of a desire to transcend as opposed to simply obtaining a "buzz," his point can still be made, although the strength of the argument is weakened. He continues that humans are "programmed to seek out nonordinary awareness, perhaps even as a way of achieving emotional equilibrium" (1987, 135). Alternatively, and contrary to the thrust of his contention, other substances and experiences have been used as a means to similar ends, sometimes in the desperate attempt to gain some relief or comfort *from* their own biology. And these are not always confused with religious experiences.

Watson takes the African context as reinforcing his position. The use of the term "supernatural" is not directly applicable to an African setting, in his estimation, since it "impl[ies] a dichotomy between the natural universe, which is subject to the laws of science; and another superimposed realm of the spirit, in which these laws do not operate." For Watson this division is a product of a Western mindset that "does not apply to African belief." Instead, the difference they envision is one between items in plain view and those which are hidden, and this does not amount to a distinction. Rather, these two "present themselves together, mixed into one common reality." This reality, according to Watson, for whom parapsychology is a favorite topic, "include[s] consciousness as an active participating factor." He is struck by the realization that recent descriptions of the world resemble the perennial philosophy or primordial tradition—the ancient "beliefs of nonliterate people" (1983, 221-22). This is not to be understood, however, in animistic terms, where the cosmos is populated with spirits, since the universe contains no divine component. In place of this, nature itself is to be accorded a high degree of admiration, bordering on reverence and veneration.

Much can be disclosed, in Watson's assessment, about conventional science in the way it treats those on its periphery. For subjects such as parapsychology, the mainstream views it as an outsider, despite the fact that it holds affiliate status (albeit grudgingly) with the American Association for the Advancement of Science since 1969. Watson uncovers the motivation behind this suspicion: "[it] is anti-materialist and a danger to the very structure of science, but ... it is impossible to identify a single law actually threatened by the reality of paranormal phenomena ... the law of Conservation of Energy and Momentum has already been broken by discoveries in quantum physics ... nothing in parapsychological discovery contradicts either the Second Law of Thermodynamics or the Principle of Causality. The only contradictions that seem to exist are with our culturally accepted view of reality based on such laws" (1987, 267).

Science, then, will only allow disciplines of a certain stripe—those that will conform to approved canons—entrance into its fold. Oddly, there appears to be a parallel here with traditionalism in theological circles. Consider this a foretaste of Part Three.

Watson's belief is that our origin is the earth, and since we came from our planet, we also mirror it. Because like generates like, we are products of the world and the two of us must resemble each other. Even the higher faculties of humans were not injected from outside, a notion to which Alfred Russell Wallace—Charles Darwin's contemporary—took the contrary position, but must stem from the same earth. (Wallace held that the human mind was a direct divine deposit; his contemporaries urged that it too was a natural product of the evolutionary process.) The fruit, naturally, does not fall far from the tree. As Watson insists, "There are levels of reality far too mysterious for totally objective common sense" (1976, 33, 40). While he may indeed have captured an essential truth here, I find that I cannot follow him in his conclusion. This is not the place to engage in arguments for and against the existence of God—that has been ably and amply treated elsewhere. Ours is the more modest, but no less profound, task of unearthing an answer to, should there be a world beyond, how it pierces through to our own? For that matter, is this even the proper question? Those and other themes will be addressed in Part Three. For now, there are three more items to tackle.

The first topic of note in the final installment of this, the shortest part of our three-part study, reintroduces a previous section. I mentioned earlier that history is written by the victors. Here is a final comment about that theme. As a prefatory statement, Watson alerts us to the belief that in evolutionary history, "a change of mind, a new idea, can have as much survival value and adaptive significance as the mutation of a gene" (1986, 11). Sometimes, though, ideas are not enough, for it depends on how they are packaged and conveyed. My parents, for example, would not branch out in terms of fast food products unless they were offered by the "safe" chain known as McDonald's. This move, in their eyes, would legitimate the product and make them feel secure—a response no doubt not lost on the marketing department of this restaurant chain. Outside of the Golden Arches lies but threatening foreign objects for my parents, suffering as they did from culinary xenophobia. McDonald's was their comfort zone. Thus new menu items may be a good idea, but for some they do not bear survival value unless they are in the proper context. One needs, therefore, to be careful when applying such notions to the arena of natural science.

Yet some innovations are of definite benefit, though they may surface from unexpected quarters. It is thought that, when successes emerge in nature, the disadvantaged are left behind. In opposition to this view, Watson has a different perspective on alleged advantage. He thinks that success can bring with it a complacency, where "all of the biggest leaps, the most profound steps, had to be taken by failures." He cites a type of "failed fish, [which] found competition too intense beneath the surface and in desperation sought refuge on land. We [humans] are all [its] descendants" (1986, 19). Contrary to Darwin, being ousted from its niche, or livelihood, did not spell extinction for this fish, since it forged for itself a new niche. What does this tell us about innovation? Well, a positive spin could be placed on Watson's tale in that no other fish was *successful* in carving out another terrestrial livelihood in the face of the "superstar" fishes. If any other species, or individual(s) within it, made the attempt, it failed. Hence in such a description, we are still referring to successes. The defeated or vanquished in one sense became the successes or victors in another. It depends on who writes the historical account—that would be us, with a failure for an ancestor.

Speaking of successes, for a second item, it is a matter of doubt as to when consciousness commenced in human life. When was it that humans first experienced the great "aha" moment when self-awareness kicked in? Was it similar to Patty Duke's portrayal of Helen Keller in the 1962 film, *The Miracle Worker*, when she finally put together the symbol for water with the object itself? When the connection was made, there was no going back. In came rushing a flood of implications as to what this breakthrough revelation held for all other symbols and their referents. Is this indicative of what occurred with our first ancestor, when primates initially rose to consciousness? How long did it take before our primogenitor noticed when staring at its reflection not only "that's me," but also lamented, "oh drat, another epidermal crease"? And how long after that did it engage in self-assessment and evaluate its current status and bemoan, "I am not reaching my full potential and have yet to become authentically self-actualized"? (Well, perhaps a while.) Nevertheless, the current treatise from the present author is a partial product of some 40,000 years of civilized reflection. And we have been making similar statements and asking similar questions ever since (without much progress).

The third and final item concerns time, and with it we mark a transition to Part Three. There are some cultures for which tenses—temporal, or time-oriented designations—are of lesser significance than in the Western world. For instance, Watson notes that "in many African languages, the same word is used for both 'yesterday' and 'tomorrow.' The present is the center of time, but distance from the present is more important than direction. Past and future are not seen as opposites, merely as more remote forms of the present. This makes the ancestors very real and well capable of exerting a profound influence over everyday activities" (1983, 118). Now neither Watson nor the Christian West espouses the active presence of ancestors or their worship, but the following can be stated about the issue of time.

The dominant religion in the West takes a bleak view of time with respect to its divinity. Temporal sequence is often pictured as unworthy of God, for the ravages of the passage of time should not touch the deity. Thus it is best to affirm that God is timeless, so the reasoning goes. If this were the case, then the sacred text of Christendom should offer clarity on this score; yet, sadly, it is lacking. Not only that, but it appears that the reverse is true. As pointed out to me by a former student of mine, Revelation 8:1 teaches that "When the Lamb opened the seventh seal, there was silence in heaven for about half an hour." The specific words selected by the author(s) were not "What seemed to be this length of time to the ordinary understanding," or "What a mere mortal could only describe as ..." To make matters worse, Revelation 22:2 intones that "the tree of life, with its twelve kinds of fruit, produc[es] its [crop] each month." Hence, according to the Christian scriptures, time in heaven, or the new heaven and the new earth, is reckoned at least in terms of hours and months. This makes even time a heavenly variable. If some commentators of this sacred text maintain that these references are largely to be interpreted metaphorically, then why stop there? The same could be argued for the remainder of the text, with drastic theological ramifications. More on time as applied to God in the pages below, but for our preliminary purposes here, at minimum it can be declared that doctrines which are considered obvious and straightforward might not only be bereft of biblical support, but the scriptures may actually militate against such views. If traditionalists imagine that divine timelessness is a biblical idea, then they will need to explain these verses.

Now that we have briefly examined the world of nature, we can turn our attention to God's relation to it. One question to focus our efforts on will be, if all of nature evolves and is thus subject to time, does this also hold true for God? In our experience, everything in time evolves. Does that mean God is necessarily placed outside of time? What are our options? These discussions bring us back squarely to the issue of God and the scriptures and whether the latter gives a faithful representation of the former.

PART THREE

Models of Divinity

Classical Theism

WE INHERIT MANY THINGS FROM OUR PARENTS—genetics sees to that. We also receive from them an early training in worldviews, that is, a perspective on the world. Before we learn to think independently, we are in the formative stages intellectually and tend to adopt uncritically the values and outlook of our parents. "If it was good enough for them,..." is often our reasoning. After all, they would not steer us wrong, would they? We do not really give it much thought.

We further receive input from our cultural environs. We become socialized into a particular way of thinking and living through the educational system and religious affiliation. We are informed by whichever structures we allow to have a shaping influence on us, and they do leave their marks. Their way of doing things becomes routine for us and assumptions become habit-forming, so much so that we cannot even envision taking on a different approach. There are parallels here with indoctrination and brainwashing.

As part of the socialization process, we are exposed to what we are supposed to think about God. Through the trust accorded to those in authority, such as the clergy, or maybe as a result of laziness or neglect on our part, we let others do some important thinking for us. We attend to the daily necessities, they take care of the eternal verities. Besides, they have resources that we could not tap in to. They seem to have access to things that are hidden from us, or to that best left undisturbed by us. They wear the mantle

85

of privileged knowledge, so we should just take their word for it. Theirs is the pipeline to a higher dimension. Better then to give them a wide berth.

When asked to describe what God might look like if a photograph could be taken of the deity, the immediate response would likely be "an old man with a long, white beard and long, flowing white robe." I suppose we have Michelangelo's painting of the creation of Adam to thank (or blame) for this. It pays to advertise. If you want to promote God to a Mediterranean crowd, then appeal to their sensibilities and market God as a Mediterranean. That will be certain to attract a following. (Although one could pose the question as to whether God really possesses a gender, a wardrobe or an age—despite being referred to, in the case of the latter, as the Ancient of Days [Daniel 7:9, 13, 22].)

And when asked to describe not God's physical but personality-type characteristics—the faculties that God exhibits—the standard list of metaphysical and moral attributes arises. It would be appropriate to devote some space to outlining these divine properties or predicates. There are about nine metaphysical and eleven moral attributes that have been assigned to the classical or traditional model of God in Christian theological history, and it is believed that they all carry biblical warrant.

First the metaphysical. These are understood as those traits that only the divinity can reflect; we cannot participate in them. They indicate a distinction between the human and divine that is impossible to bridge. They include the following:

1) *Independence*—The divinity is self-existent in the sense that God's being derives from God's self. God does not require any outside sources in order to exist. The same cannot be said for us, because we are needy creatures and require food, shelter and clothing for survival. We are not able to endure for long periods without water or air before we perish. Not so for the deity. There is also a related sense in which God is independent. God is self-sufficient and does not need to be provided with anything, physical or otherwise, least of all from the world that God created. God could do just fine without it, thank you very much.

(Some of the biblical passages that are referred to in support of this view include John 5:26; Acts 17:25; and Romans 11:35.)

2) *Spirituality*—Building on the first theme, God is pure spirit without any physical or corporeal aspects. This is just as well, since if God did, then God would not be independent—the part of God which was not spirit, like other physical objects, would require care and attention. Herein lies a problem, however. This category cannot readily apply to the alleged second member or person of the Trinity, since he spent his entire earthly ministry being physical. If Jesus is God, then God had at least thirty years of familiarity with life on this planet as a human. Unless of course one adopts the gnostic posture which hails Jesus as a type of Hindu avatar or phantom, where he is merely in the form of a human, but is not fully human. He would then be more like a projection or hologram than actual flesh and blood.

(Examples: John 4:24; 1 Timothy 1:17, 6:16.)

3) *Eternality*—By the above reasoning, if God is not mortal, then God is necessarily immortal. Since nothing could cause the immortal to decay or disintegrate, then God must also be eternal—God could never not exist. Some distinctions of concepts would be in order here. It would be nice if there were to be consensus in the use of these terms, but alas, there is not. Let us employ them in the following ways for our purposes. For some theologians, eternal refers to timelessness—meaning removed from or outside of time. God would then neither be subject to time nor be affected by its passage. Another interpretation of eternal is having neither beginning nor end. With this conception, there never was a time when God was not, nor will there ever be a time when God is not. Finally, everlasting can mean unending, but there would have been a beginning. While this would not apply to God, it would apply to humans who had a beginning but will allegedly have an enduring existence either with or apart from God. The scriptures themselves are not consistent with these usages and can tend to employ them interchangeably. (There is also an indication that not even heaven, together presumably with its most notable oc-

cupant, is entirely without some time frame, as was reported at the end of Part Two.)

(Examples: Genesis 21:33; Deuteronomy 33:27; Psalm 90:2, 102:12; Isaiah 57:15.)

4) *Simplicity*—This is not a straightforward one and lacks ample biblical reinforcement. It refers to God as simple, that is, not composed of parts and free from division. God is one, a unity, without any components, whereas we are compounds—containing multiple organs for many functions. An inference is being made here, though, in greater measure than with the other attributes. It is generally agreed that this is predicated of God in a way that is more a product of philosophical commitment and presupposition than explicit scriptural statement.

(Examples: Deuteronomy 6:4; 2 Corinthians 1:19)

5) *Immutability*—Here God is said to undergo no alteration. God does not change from moment to moment, but always remains the same. So God is constant, but in what respect? God is forever unchanging in terms of God's nature, character and intentions, although these tend to experience some modification as well. (As will be presented below, God seems to adopt a different strategy periodically.) Yet are these the only possible ways to change? Can change occur in other ways, such as emotively? This brings us to our next attribute.

(Examples: Numbers 23:19; Psalm 33:11, 102:27; Malachi 3:6; Hebrews 6:17; James 1:17.)

(An instance to the contrary is Jeremiah 18:1-11, where twice it states that God will change God's mind depending on whether a nation or kingdom is obedient to God's decrees.)

6) *Impassibility*—The answer to the previous question for traditional classical theists is no. God does not emote, so this becomes another way that God does not change. God is unmoved by what occurs in the world and is passionless toward it. What good would it be, it is argued, if God were moody? This could only reflect poorly on a divinity who is supposed to be rock steady in all respects. God has no emotional investment in the world and so

can never be disappointed. Moods change, so God cannot have them. And that's that.

(Examples of this do not abound, but one to the contrary is Jeremiah 8:21-22, where it states that God is hurt, dismayed and mourns over the transgressions committed and the calamity experienced by God's people.)

7) *Omnipresence*—Much like in eternality, where God is not limited by time, here God is not limited by space. God is not bounded by any coordinate system but is present throughout space. God is everywhere that there is a place to be. There is nowhere where God is not (with the possible exception of hell).

(Examples: 1 Kings 8:27; Psalm 139:7-10; Jeremiah 23:23-24.)

8) *Omniscience*—This is the one that Pickover has the most fun with. Here God knows all that there is to know. God knows the past, present and future completely. There is nothing that is not on God's radar. In addition to knowing all actual things, God knows all possible things as well (such as whether a bunted baseball would have rolled foul if a pitcher or baseman had not intervened).

(Examples: Psalm 139:1-4; Isaiah 40:13-14, 28, 46:10; Romans 11:33.)

9) *Omnipotence*—Together with being all-present and all-knowing, God is also all-powerful. There is nothing God cannot do, provided it is consistent with God's nature, character and intentions, and that it not be logically contradictory. This later condition was an innovation supplied by Thomas Aquinas, meaning, for instance, that the logical impossibility of creating a square circle is not a knock on God's power. Omnipotence is not threatened by this inability, for it is not a possible ability, meaning it is not a requirement that God needs to meet. Nothing then can frustrate or thwart the fulfilment of the divine will.

(Examples: Genesis 18:14; 2 Chronicles 20:6; Psalm 147:5; Isaiah 14:27, 43:13; Jeremiah 32:17; Daniel 4:35; Mark 10:27; Ephesians 1:19-20.)

Having surveyed the metaphysical attributes of the classical God, we can now focus our attention on listing their moral counterparts. These are character qualities that humans can also exemplify and perhaps this is part of what it means to be created in God's image. They comprise the following, in alphabetical order: faithfulness, goodness, grace, holiness, justice, love, mercy, patience, righteousness, truthfulness and wisdom. Not only can humans participate in these, but God calls us to reflect them in increasing measure. When we are mandated to follow God, the process of becoming more like God means to produce fruit in the form of these values.

In my not having included a description of each of these moral predicates of God, the assumption is that none is required, since they convey the conventional dictionary definitions. Yet this raises the question as to whether we can be so cavalier. In philosophical terms, we can ask if they are univocal, that is, do they have precisely the same meaning in reference to God as they do for us? Is human love, for instance, the same thing as divine love? The common Greek in which the New Testament was written may reveal how impoverished the English language is in comparison, at least in this case. The Greek has four terms for love; the English only one. One of the Greek terms is reserved for the love of God; the others for types of human love. Thus it appears that a distinction does need to be made at times. Divine love is different both in degree from human love, for it is much greater or has a much greater carrying capacity, but for the Greeks it is also different in kind.

Whatever the attribute under examination, then, there are a host of biblical references that are adduced in support of their pertinence for God. Further questions, though, surface at this point. Initially, do these scripture passages actually reinforce the attribute under consideration or can another interpretation be given? Moreover, how many references are required before we can be confident that they may be applied to God? Do they at some point reach a critical mass so that they become definitive divine properties? In addition, do some passages count for more? Are they weightier, for instance, if Jesus is alleged to have uttered them?

Are they all on an equal footing, or are some more valuable than others? The way in which we answer these questions for ourselves will reveal to us the approach that we take toward the scriptures and whether we believe they could stand some renovation.

Some further comments on the ground we have just covered. To begin with, while the eleven moral attributes seem to have multiple attestations in the biblical text, the same cannot be said for the nine metaphysical ones. Only two, as it turns out—God as eternal and spirit—have direct scriptural referent. The others are inferred. The prefix omni-, for example, appears nowhere in the translation of the Bible that we are using here, namely the New Revised Standard Version (NRSV). This means that a framework has been placed on the statements in order to make sense of them. This organizational tactic, however, could backfire if the statements are being stretched inappropriately. Where do these ideas originate, then? They are Greek categories about which we will have more to say below. But for now, we can mention that over time it has become an assumption that Christians should adopt this Greek way of thinking, for such notables as Augustine and Aquinas were impressed with Greek philosophy and imagined that this would be a good way to systematize and frame the Christian message. So if it was good enough for them, then who are we to argue? Yet I see no reason for being committed to this line of thinking. This may be the legacy we have inherited, but the assumption that to be Christian means to conceive of God in this way is not a requirement. If the ancient Greeks insist on working with this type of divinity, then that is fine; they are welcome to do so. Carry on. Yet I feel no compulsion to entertain these thought forms just because some ancient Greek guy recommends it. I would rather see the full menu. And we will consider two alternatives in due course.

Some final thoughts before we switch our focus. As some philosophers and systematic theologians maintain, the metaphysical attributes of God do not hang together well as they stand, for they do not form a coherent whole. One example of internal inconsistency is the combination of omniscience and omnipotence. If God knows everything completely, including the future, then this places a constraint on God's power. For if the future is settled, then God does not have the power to alter it, should God ever desire to do so. The issue here is not interest but ability—this is not something that God can accomplish. The reverse also holds true. If God is all-powerful, then the future can be changed, which leaves God without the standard notion of omniscience. The Greeks have painted God into a corner—God cannot be omniscient and omnipotent at the same time.

But the difficulties do not end there. Particularly in reference to Jesus, the attributes begin to show signs of fragility. As humans cannot participate in the metaphysical attributes, this also leaves Jesus out. To those who regard Jesus as having two natures—human and divine —(which was not accepted as official doctrine until the council of Nicea in 325 CE) these predicates begin to crumble. For starters, a human is not independent, even if he happens to be Jesus. According to the mythical accounts, only Adam and Eve arrived on the scene without mothers. Spirituality is also sacrificed, since humans are unbendingly corporeal. By our definition, neither can Jesus be eternal since he had a beginning. Jesus cannot be immutable, since there was a time when he was not human—indicative of a major change. Nor was he impassible, for he undertook his Passion and also longed to gather Jerusalem's children as a hen gathers her chicks (Matthew 23: 37; Luke 13:34). (Notice the female imagery, suggesting that God should not be thought of purely in male terms.) Jesus was not omnipresent, since he was confined to the Ancient Near East. Neither was he omniscient, for only the Father knows the time of Jesus' return (Matthew 24:36; Mark 13:32). Nor did he have personal experience of what it is like to grow old. And lastly, Jesus was not omnipotent, for he could not do (many) mighty works in his home country because of the people's lack of faith (Matthew 13:53-58; Mark 6:1-6). At best, then, it seems that the metaphysical attributes do not apply to the second member of the Trinity, but mainly to the other two. And this is where my final point comes in. Notice that I left out one of those predicates. If God exists in three Persons— a doctrine not approved until the council of Constantinople in 381 CE—then God is also not simple, but a compound. God is made up of parts—a membership or set of three in the Godhead. Not just different hats or masks to wear or roles to play but three Persons. Hence all the attributes fall at certain points.

Is the Bible For or Against Theology?

Regrettably, the Bible does not prove to be helpful on all counts. On theological fronts, the sought after clarity sometimes fails to materialize. Here is a case in point. In certain Christian circles, another theological issue arises, concerning not only who God is but what God does. There is a divide between two camps on the themes of divine election and human perseverance. The first deals with the question of God's selection of who is to be given the gift of salvation, or saving faith, and what it depends on. That is, the choice as to who to include in God's salvation program and how God arrives at these results. The second addresses the problem of whether it is possible to forfeit this gift once it has been received. Will the recipients forever remain in that state after it has been obtained or is there a danger that a redeemed person can irreversibly fall away or become irretrievably lost? Is the offer good once and for all, or is there a risk involved? The two camps are the Calvinist/Reformed and the Arminian/Wesleyan. Some denominations which usually bear these names include the Dutch or Christian Reformed, the Presbyterian and the Congregationalist over against the Methodist, respectively.

The trouble is, in the first instance, that there seem to be as many scripture passages that indicate certain selected humans as appointed for salvation (examples: John 15:16; Acts 13:48; Romans 8:29; Ephesians 1:4) and about which we have no choice or say in the matter, as there are those verses which imply that the onus is on us (examples: Ezekiel 33:11; Mark 1:15; Acts 7:51; 1 Timothy 2:3-4) and that we must do all we can to heed the gospel message. An equal amount suggest that God is the only player involved in who becomes the recipient of God's saving grace, as those which claim that the selection process is not a foregone conclusion. In the second case, there appear to be as many references to redemption as forever secure (examples: John 6:39, 10:28-29; Romans 8:38-39; Philippians 1:6; 2 Timothy 1:12, 4:18) and about which we can be confident, as there are those verses which indicate that there is a genuine peril in the calculations (examples: John 15:6; Romans 11:22; Colossians 1;23; 1 Timothy 1:19; Hebrews 3:14, 6:4-6; 2 Peter 2:20-21) and that we need to be careful to exercise caution, be ever vigilant and keep up our end of the bargain. These are often stated as conditionals, namely, "if you do not remain or endure, then you will be cut off." Once again, our final state would appear to be dependent upon how we carry out our calling. Should our faith become "shipwrecked," then there is no going back. We cannot be brought back to our previous status, and it would have been better had we never agreed to it in the first place. If we turn our back on it, "then we are worse off at the end than we were at the beginning."

One might claim, in response, that different biblical authors have different emphases, thereby covering all the theological bases and together describing the whole of God's strategy. Yet interestingly, sometimes conflicting messages come from the same biblical book or author (examples: John, Acts, Romans, 2 Timothy) when the above lists are compared. Whence then the discrepancy? Why must the Bible be so ambiguous? We approach the scriptures for answers, but at times the desired clarity becomes elusive and is unavailable. The biblical statements are emphatic in each case— insisting that this is the way it is. But the way things are is at least twofold. So which way is right? Can only one way be right? How do we choose? This evidently calls for wisdom to unravel the mystery. But it makes the task of systematic theology very difficult, for mixed messages do not easily conform to one system, one neat package. It thus becomes impossible to believe the entirety of this sacred text, for some portions of it will militate against one's outlook and set up a contrary position. It is at these very points where one must admit that one does not follow the entirety of the Bible's teaching. In this way we exhibit our own biases. We prefer our own way of thinking to that of the full biblical witness. Yet take heart, for there is really no getting around it. An outbreak of clear thought will reveal that the sooner we become comfortable with the tension and live with the ambiguity of the Bible, the better off we will be.

If additional convincing is required, then consider another example. The sacred text of the Christians is not even clear with regard to the issue of the onset of Jesus' having become the Son of God. When do the scriptures mention its having commenced? The search for an answer does not disappoint. On the contrary, there are too many of them. Let us survey the evidence not in the order in which it appears according to the table of contents for the New Testament, but in chronological order—the order in which the writings likely emerged in literary history.

The first indication comes from an alleged writing of the apostle Paul—the letter to the Romans. In the introductory section of this epistle (1:4), Paul states that Jesus has been "declared to be Son of God ... by [his] resurrection from the dead." Prior to this time, apparently, the jury was still out. It took the resurrection event to seal the deal. The second stems from what is taken to be the oldest canonical gospel. In Mark 1:9-11, Jesus presents himself to John the Baptist for baptism. When the rite was completed, a voice from heaven spoke to him, informing him that he is the Father's Beloved Son, with whom God is "well pleased." The gospel of Matthew has a slightly different spin on this episode. The voice that came from heaven is directed not to Jesus himself but to those in attendance, as a proud father would introduce a son in whom he delights (3:17).

Next comes the gospel of Luke, which places the onset of Jesus' Sonship even prior to his conception. Mary is approached by the angel Gabriel who informs her that the child that she is soon to carry "will be called the Son of the Most High" (1:31-35). Finally, in John's gospel, Jesus, according to some interpreters, is identified with the Word or wisdom of God, who was with God and was God from the beginning (1:1-18). This Word became flesh, but also created the world. Hence Jesus was God's Son from before the foundation of the world.

Thus it appears that the later the New Testament document, the earlier Jesus is seen as wearing the mantle of God's Son in it. As time goes on, the divinity of Jesus is pushed further back. In this case, then, the scriptures provide us with more answers than we asked for, and might even be prepared for. Hence the answer to the question as to when Jesus became God's Son is "that depends on which biblical passage you refer to." There are at least four different responses. Different authors have different takes on it.

Another example derives from human (mis)deeds together with expectations of rewards or punishments. It was thought, in the ancient Near East, that God's covenants reflected God's justice; if one entered into these contracts, then the two parties knew what to expect. God demands fidelity and obedience to God's laws and decrees on the part of the people, and if these conditions are met, then the arrangement stipulates that the people would benefit. There were no surprises. Fulfillment of commands meant prosperity from the God who offers it. These blessings were understood to be in the form of individual longevity, perhaps even combined with land and other possessions. The book of Proverbs suggests that there is a one-to-one correspondence of actions and consequences and this became conventional wisdom. You get what you deserve. And we continue to think along these lines. If someone prospers, we might declare "You must live right," as if to say that the fates reward the taking of a straight path.

Not everything turned out to be so obvious, however. The author of the book of Ecclesiastes notes that, in a counterintuitive way, sometimes the wicked prosper and the righteous are afflicted. So much for conventional wisdom. Then along comes the book of Job, which tackles the problem of evil head on. Job experienced unjust suffering, though he never charged God with wrongdoing. As a result, Job was rewarded with greater blessings at the end than he had originally, albeit the route to get there was tragic, as it involved the untimely deaths of his offspring. Yet no explanation is given as to why there is evil. In chapters 38 to 41, God speaks from the whirlwind and asks Job "Who are you to cast aspersions on my economy?" It seems like that is something we simply need to live with. Job's question, "Why me?" is never satisfactorily answered.

Then finally arrives the book of Daniel, the latter half of which is taken to be the most recent of the Old Testament documents—written likely during the Maccabean revolt period of 175-160 BCE. Herein the thorny question gets answered. In Daniel 12:1-2, we are informed that the dead will rise again, and there is the insight. If God's justice appears suspect in this life, then the afterlife will attend to it. Prior to this time, the Jews did not really entertain a view of the hereafter. They envisioned what they referred to as Sheol—a gloomy place with an equally uninviting existence attached to it. Definitely not an improvement over earthly life. One did not wish to hasten toward this destination. But if the dead will arise, then there would be another opportunity for setting things right. That was the advantage of this approach—inequities had a chance to be revisited and grievances redressed. Here would be the time and place for judgment and final rewards or punishments. Hence this is how God's justice was viewed from one Old Testament period to the next. It too experienced a development, or evolution, in subsequent biblical treatments.

So the Bible is not always as helpful as we would hope. There is an age-old question that Christian theologians have addressed in the history of Christian thought, and that is what is to be the final arbiter or court of appeal when an issue is to be settled—philosophy or the scriptures? The answer now seems clearer—it depends which philosophy and which part of the biblical text one has in view.

Laying the Foundation

If I were to be receiving treatment from a psychiatrist, I might begin the session with "The problem started with..." or "The difficulty began with..." If I were to be a detective, I might be inclined to announce that "We have a suspect in custody," or "We think we have found the culprit." Mine is the more forensic declaration of "We have secured a fingerprint—lifted it right off the root issue." For here is where the early Christian theologians left their mark, or more accurately, found a philosophical home. This is the ground upon which Christian thinking has laid a foundation, and the structure that was built upon it has endured for two millennia. Yet cracks appear in it and the edifice is in danger of crumbling.

I speak of ancient Greek philosophy. These fellows (for there was nary a woman amongst them invited to the inner circle) decided that God should be understood as being what the world is not. Whatever characteristics the world displays is to have its opposing counterparts in the divine. It was noticed that the world exhibits change, which by the Greek philosophers was perceived in negative terms. Change, they saw, led ultimately to degeneration, hence they coined the saying "change implies corruptibility." The list of traits the world presents came to include such concepts as mutability or changeableness, mobility, potentiality, passivity, temporality and, of course, materiality. Only changing things are subject to corruption; thus the world is noted for its becoming. God, on the other hand, must exemplify those attributes in stark and utter contrast to the world. Since God is nothing like the world, God must be immutable, immobile, actual, active, eternal and incorporeal— the exact opposite in each case. Only God is incorruptible, so the divinity cannot change. God is thereby noted for being static, or more precisely, is known as static being. God is known for permanence, the world for impermanence.

Value judgments can then be attached to these sets of terms. The static is appraised as highly valued for its incorruptibility; the changing world is devalued for its corruptibility. God and the noncorporeal realm are therefore judged as good; the corporeal world evil. This dichotomy is referred to as dualistic, since all of reality is divided into two opposing camps. Anything physical, including (non-contemplative) humans, is looked down upon; anything spiritual is elevated. For Aristotle, matter is believed to be composed of substance and form. Only God is pure form. Hence God has no substance and thus cannot be material.

The world reveals imperfections, so God must possess only perfections. This list of perfections is the list of divine attributes of the classical tradition outlined above. They amount to a perfect being and this is the root of the concern. The Christian world was influenced by this mode of thinking and sought to frame its own view of God and the world in these terms. Consequently, God came to be seen as unconditional, meaning God is independent. The God of Aristotle is a necessary being and is dubbed the Unmoved Mover. In terms that we have already encountered, God's unmoved nature can be understood in two ways: constitutionally, making God immutable; and emotionally, making God impassible. Further, God has no internal division and is therefore simple. Christian conceptions of God can be traced back to the ancient Greek philosophical world. The early Christian thinkers were impressed with this perfect being theology and desired that their God bear these marks as well.

This is where the issues emerge. From the inception of Christian metaphysical speculation, it was reasoned that God shows providential care for the creation. As a result, this must be incorporated into theology. The trouble is that what one divine attribute affirms, another denies. Independence and providence, to take one case, cannot really stand together. One cannot both care and be self-sufficient, since the expression of care indicates some dependence on the one cared for. The state of the object of one's care becomes the condition for the state of the subject. Care for a loved one will affect one's emotional state. And if one cares, then one has emotional investment in someone or something else; and this constitutes something other than independence. Moreover, care entails changes in the way that this providence is exercised, for it depends on the changing state of the recipient. If the object changes, so too does the response of the subject. Let us assess the ground we have just covered. At a stroke, the divine attributes of independence, impassibility and immutability are now suspect, or even in jeopardy—all with the insistence that God cares! If we want to uphold a providential God, the cost will be this set of three attributes.

Later theological debates in Christian history were to involve additional perplexing issues. Recalling a previous theme, when the doctrine of Jesus as having two natures was given official approbation, this implied that physicality is not foreign to the divine. If Jesus is both human and divine, then by definition the attribute of spirituality cannot be retained, for the scriptures teach that Jesus both came in the flesh and now enjoys a resurrected body. Next, when it became apparent that the New Testament describes three divine figures, the doctrine of the Trinity gained support and was finally recognized as orthodox and received into the tradition. What this connotes, however, is that God is made up of parts, namely, there is God the Father, God the Son and God the Holy Spirit. Having divisions yields a God who is not simple but complex. The Christian God is now a compound—comprised of Three Persons. This became a concern for those who wished to promote monotheism—consistent with the Jewish tradition—and avoid polytheism, meaning that there is now a fourth attribute in peril. That makes four out of nine metaphysical attributes that have fallen in short order.

Preliminary conclusions: We should not allow an ancient Greek philosopher to set the agenda or to do our thinking for us; and God may very well be unlike the God of both the Greeks as well as of the biblical text.

Father Knows Best?

As before, the problems do not end there but are compounded. The dilemma becomes what should one retain or discard? The Hebrew-Hellenic philosopher Philo, as well as the Church Fathers through to Augustine (see Figure 3), dealt with these very themes. Their and our discussion now expands into the three omni's. Early Christian thinkers such as Augustine believed God to witness history from the perspective of an eternal present. That is, God sees all of time from the same time. There are no past, present or future distinctions for God, but all of time is equally present for the divine. Nor can this panorama undergo alteration. If everything is plainly within God's purview, then this vantage point represents an immutable vision—one which cannot change. If God is able to catch sight of all of time in an instant, then the particulars of what we experience as the passage of time are all settled events for God. If the deity's vision cannot change, neither can the events themselves, since they are what God sees.

This brings up some troubling implications. As the set of three attributes mentioned above is connected, meaning if one topples, then the others are likewise affected or put at risk (like a domino effect), so too is there a second set of three. In the way that fragility about impassibility leads to the same for independence, which, in turn, leads to putting immutability on the spot, a similar progression obtains for omnipotence, omniscience and free will. While we have not included free will as a divine metaphysical attribute, since, unlike the other ones, we believe we can participate in it as well, it remains an alleged faculty on God's part as it does for us. We may be deluded in this, but it continues to be a strong perception on our part, one that resists being ignored.

With omniscience, there is no event which awaits determination for God. Nothing is conditional or contingent—the future is as determined as the past and present. This means no modifications can ever occur, even were it to please God to effect them. Since the classical God is understood to be active rather than passive, and that no other being can exceed God in supremacy, for then God would not be supreme, God would be guilty of being the architect of the history that God perceives. To employ another metaphor, God not only witnesses events but, using this reasoning, must also have engineered them. Who else could have authored them if not the cosmic C.E.O.? If this were true, if God not only views history but makes it, then we are left with the odious realization that God must have drawn up the plans for the Holocaust, for that is part of the history that God sees and has fashioned.

We are led to this conclusion because the history that God sees cannot change, otherwise it could not properly be known beforehand. If God were to know a future that changes, then God's initial knowledge is faulty. For a changing knowledge would make an eternal knowledge erroneous. Besides, why would God entertain a change of plans instead of getting it right the first time, from the outset of the world? Consequently, if God happens to enjoy free will, God cannot exercise it in an already settled history. Our belief that we have it would then also be illusory. Nor can God do anything about history—the issue turning now from interest to ability. God has no power over the future, even if God wanted to modify it. An omniscient God cannot intervene, for then the future that God knows would become altered. What strikes us is that both free will and omnipotence are incompatible with the type of omniscience that includes the future. At most, one could establish two of the three, but there would be no room for the third (Pickover, 144-45).

If the above reasoning is accurate, then a full two-thirds of the metaphysical attributes are in critical condition (and tack on free will for good measure). These are but some of the internal inconsistencies of the traditional model of deity, which cannot bear up under the weight of its own shortcomings. The other attributes crumble in reference to Jesus as having the dual natures of humanity and divinity. To the extent that Jesus is corporeal, God is not entirely spirit; and as the human Jesus is finite and in time, God is not completely eternal (or timeless, at least). Indeed, the metaphysical attributes fail to apply as much to the human Jesus as to us and the rest of the world. If God is what the world is not, then Jesus is unlike God. Some have claimed that if we want to know what God is like, all we need to do is look at Jesus. Though by our rationale, we are no closer to a glimpse of God in this way. If Jesus is the Way, he cannot be the view, for God is different from the world.

There seem to be only two options open to us. Either we reject, together with the Arians, the idea that Jesus can be God, as the physical can be spiritual, or the finite infinite, etc., or we deny, unlike the Greeks, that God must be totally dissimilar to the world. Before we can proceed, we need to regain our footing and our bearings, else we run aground.

Other Roads

We can best obtain an overview of alternatives to the classical model by situating the latter along a spectrum, which is provided in Figure 1. In terms of God's relation to the world, the traditional approach can be placed on one extreme of the axis. Setting it on the right suggests that it represents a conservative leaning, although each movement has its left and right wings. It will be noted that there are actually two positions on the right end. The one on the far right portrays a situation where there is a complete separation between God and the world, with the divine residing above the line and drawn as an inverted parabola. This connotes an infinite aspect to God, while the world or universe below the line is depicted as a closed circle, thereby conveying its finitude (albeit perhaps immense in proportion). The separation implies that God is removed from the world and not (or no longer) involved in it. And the placement of God above the line intimates God's total transcendence to the world. This rendering has been described by some theologians and religious philosophers as God being "wholly other," meaning entirely different in regards to the world (Soren Kierkegaard, Rudolf Otto), or "over against the world as its Creator" (Karl Barth). God is distinct from the world and fully unlike it. This viewpoint would play into the hands of the Greek dualists. And in certain moments, this strategy is referred to as deism.

FIGURE 1
God's Relation to the World

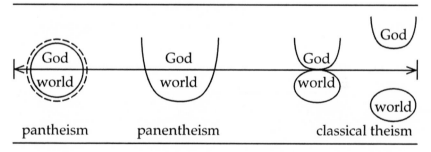

pantheism   panentheism   classical theism

To be fair, there are complexions of classical theism which do admit of or make allowances for a point or points of contact. This is where the near right position comes in. The divine and the world touch at the level of the line and this intersection point affirms an ongoing presence of God in the world. This limited immanence can take the following shapes (and there are others). There is, according to this theological tradition, an enduring fingerprint of God in that humans are understood to be created in God's image. A lasting presence is also purported in some circles to reside in the sacrament known as the Eucharist. And most importantly,

God is said to have become human in the form of Jesus, with Jesus continuing to carry with Him a transformed kind of corporeality known as a resurrection body. While it is not certain as to how this connection could be made, there appears to be an analogous situation in the human mind-body/brain problem. As it is unclear how something mental can affect something physical, such as the intent to raise an arm becoming translated into that very same physical act, so too is it mysterious as to how the spiritual can influence the material. Mentality is nothing like physicality (as Rene Descartes recognized in what could be called the "classical Cartesian conundrum"), although the two are allegedly connected, nor is spirituality at all similar to materiality, although one might find its origins in the other. The two issues, I propose, are related. Making progress in one could spill over into the other. Advancements in one could go a long way toward unravelling the mystery of the other. It is for this reason that the mind-body/brain problem can be called the God-world relation in miniature.

At the opposite pole from classical theism resides the pantheist position. "Pan" means "everything" in Greek and "theos" refers to God; hence everything *is* God. Thus God and the world are superimposed in a sense. One is equivalent to and identified with the other. In contrast to the traditional extreme, God is entirely immanent in the world at this end. Whereas in the classical view there is a metaphysics of dualism, here there is one of monism. All of reality is composed of one substance—either matter, as in materialism, or mind, as in idealism. Hence there is a movement from total separation of God and the world to complete identification as one proceeds toward the left. There is a decision that needs to be made at this point, however, by those who favor the pantheistic approach. If God is all, then there must be a consonance between God and the world when it comes to scale. If one insists on a finite universe, then God must also be finite; if the cosmos can safely be regarded as infinite, then so may God.

Fortunately, perhaps, there is also at least one mediating position between these two extremes. This is the camp of process thought. Here God dips below the line so as to include the world, making this a panentheistic perspective, where reality is comprised of everything *in* God (the "en" between "pan" and "theistic" simply means "in"). God is thereby the total reality, part of which is the world of nature. God equals the world but is infinitely more than the world. This is very much a both-and approach, whereas the extremes are either-or. In this inclusive strategy, there is both transcendence and immanence. The perception from the middle is that each extreme is partially or half right, but incomplete on its own. In this view, everything is internal to God: the finite part of God that is the world is the embodied aspect of God, constituting (after a fashion) God's body, and the infinite aspect of God serves (so to speak) as God's mind. The world is internal to God while God is also external to the world, but now the world of physics and the realm of metaphysics are reunited in one reality which is God, who contains the many. On the right side of the spectrum there are two things, as the dualists would have it: mind and body or spirit and matter. On the left there is only one thing, as the monists would declare: physicality or mentality. In the middle there is only one thing but with two moments or modes of expression, making it a dipolar scheme (Hartshorne, 1984).

One final note. The right half of the spectrum yields another spectrum, which is shown in Figure 2. This does not include the left half of the previous one because pantheism is not usually taken as a Christian concept of God as such. This statement should not be construed as reflecting judgmentality, however, for

FIGURE 2
Christian Concepts of God

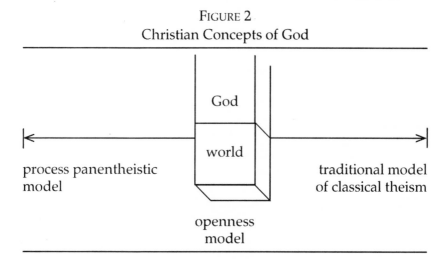

process panentheistic
model

traditional model
of classical theism

openness
model

by their own admission pantheists would not generally declare themselves to be Christian. (The Christian message for the *world* does not need to be extended to *God*. If God is the world and the world needs salvation, then so too does God.) The three models of divinity that together form the basis of this investigation occupy positions along this latter spectrum. Classical theism remains on the far right; process panentheism, formerly in the middle in Figure 1, is now on the far left here in Figure 2; and the openness model (to be covered last) lies somewhere in between.

It might also be helpful to situate the main players in these philosophical and theological exercises, and for this reason Figure 3 supplies a cursory historical outline. Here the time line extends from earliest at the top to more recent at the bottom. Greek thinking, as was mentioned, constitutes the groundwork of these discussions, for better or for worse. Hence Socrates appears at the

FIGURE 3
Historical Outline of Theological Traditions

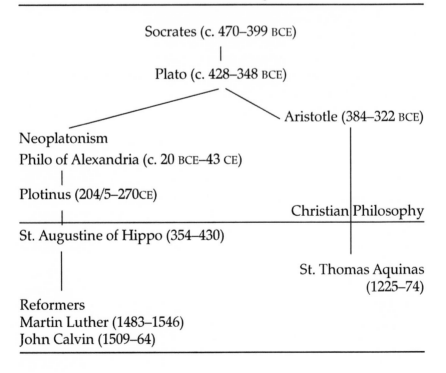

Socrates (c. 470–399 BCE)

|

Plato (c. 428–348 BCE)

Aristotle (384–322 BCE)

Neoplatonism
Philo of Alexandria (c. 20 BCE–43 CE)

|

Plotinus (204/5–270CE)

Christian | Philosophy

St. Augustine of Hippo (354–430)

St. Thomas Aquinas
(1225–74)

Reformers
Martin Luther (1483–1546)
John Calvin (1509–64)

top, even though there were philosophers prior to him, known (unimaginatively) as the Pre-Socratics, followed by his most famous student, Plato, who acts as a mouthpiece for his teacher in the Platonic dialogues. The stream branches into two from this point. One tradition leads through Aristotle, Plato's most famous student, to the Doctor of the Catholic Church—St. Thomas Aquinas, who was a Dominican monk. The other leads through Neo-platonism, meaning a new form of Platonic thought, to a number of later thinkers. Stops along the way include Philo of Alexandria (who wanted to add providential care onto an independent divinity), Plotinus (to be examined next), St. Augustine (who stressed the immutable vision of God's eternal present, where all of time is now to God), and finally to the Protestant Reformers such as Martin Luther and John Calvin.

In the case of the latter, sometimes an advance is actually a retreat. By this I mean that their emphasis was the idea of "getting back to the Bible," where they urged that their heroes of the faith, who would serve this purpose, were men like Augustine. The Reformers believed that some of the essentials of the tradition were lost in the intervening time between Augustine and the soon to become Protestant Reformation movement. They sought to revive these essentials in and for their own age. Their battle cry became "sola scriptura," meaning the scriptures alone. Needless to say, on the issue of philosophy versus the sacred text, the Reformers would insist that too much stress has been laid upon philosophy and it was time to push for a change (though their practice did not always match their theory). The tradition, for them, had lost sight of biblical wisdom and it needed to refocus. Reference will also be made to a certain heretical movement (so-called), known as the Socinians, who maintained that Augustine's teaching was overrated by the Reformers.

An Emanating Deity

(The influence, inspiration, and not a little of the content, for this and the next several sections is the 1953 edited work by Charles

Hartshorne and William L. Reese entitled *Philosophers Speak of God*.) Before we embark on an investigation of pantheism, it is worth having a look at the "emanationism" of Plotinus. His view of God is analogous to a mountain, or better yet, a volcano, where God resides at the summit and everything in existence emanates from God as lava flows down the slopes of a volcano. The further removed something is from the summit, the more a material object it becomes. And as a corollary, the closer something is to God, which Plotinus calls the One, the more like God it becomes. As one travels down the slope, one encounters mind, consciousness and then the world of matter. Contrary to the Greek dualistic universe of thinkers like Plato, however, everything in reality for Plotinus is good, since it all stems from the One. This marks a major difference from dualism, which did not have a high regard for the material world. This is one of the reasons that Plotinus is a Neoplatonist—he forges a new type of Platonism.

The path down the slope constitutes a descent, though this is not to be interpreted in terms of a value judgment. The progression from the One to the many does yield a movement from the superior to the inferior, yet this does not amount to a degeneration. Unity produces multiplicity, but the complexity thus engendered is not viewed in a negative light. After all, everything has the same source. And it becomes the task for humans, even our religious duty, to make our way back to the One at the top through the exercise of contemplation.

An interesting question to pose to Plotinus at this point concerns the very world at the base of this volcano, namely, is the world that emanates from God a necessary or a contingent product? Does it issue forth automatically from the One or is it conditional upon other factors, such as divine choice? It seems that there are three possibilities, which are highlighted in Figure 4. Firstly, if it is conceded that the world is dependent upon the will of God, who freely creates the world, then there might never have been a world at all, let alone this one. Hence both the world and its particulars arise from the divinity. This world is thus external to God and the deity's simplicity is preserved. We have seen this position before—it goes by the name of classical theism.

The second option, at the opposite extreme, which is likely the one Plotinus himself would have endorsed, is having the world necessarily stem from God—so that it becomes entirely dependent on God while also being independent of free will, for God had no choice in the matter. On a point to be explained momentarily, the world is then internal to God; yet this entails that God's simplicity cannot be retained concurrently. If the One contains the many, then it is really complex after all. This perspective also has a name—it is known as pantheism, the position to be discussed next. There is also a mediating alternative. The stance in the middle sees the world as necessary but its details as contingent, which means they could have been different. Once again, the world would be internal to God, who loses or forfeits simplicity. This is called the process panentheistic scheme. But look where we have come. The three possibilities that our question has yielded amount to the three options from Figure 1. The alternatives reduce to the spectrum of positions on God's relation to the world. This implies that on the issue of God as cause of the world, Plotinus is left without a stance of his own, for the three available ones have already been taken (Hartshorne & Reese, 76-84).

God as the World

Allow us now to have a closer look at the pantheistic tradition of Spinoza (1632-77). This Jewish Dutchman wrestled with the classical theism of his day. Using the chart from Figure 4, we can begin to make sense of the source of his disquiet. The main concern for Spinoza is that he could not tolerate the idea that a contingent world would not also affect a non-contingent divinity, thereby making God contingent as well. The recourse is to hold firm to the classical picture which paints the deity as both necessary and omniscient. Yet the implication of this reasoning is that the world is predetermined. To have a complete knowledge of the future, as admitted before, means that the future has been mapped out—planned from the outset. More precisely, the order for God is in the reverse direction: since the future is foreordained, this enables

FIGURE 4

Theological Commitments on the Issue of the World as
Caused by God Necessarily or Contingently

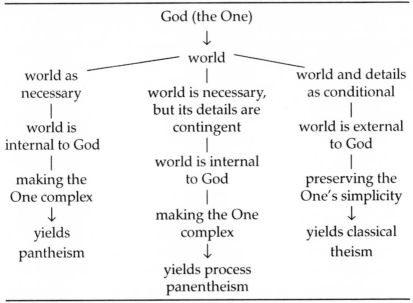

God to know it completely. A predestined future gives God the knowledge of it. The philosophical move which Spinoza now makes is that if we accept the foregoing, then there is nothing preventing us from transplanting the world from God's external to God's internal environment. A world that is now internal to God is rendered as necessary as God is; the reason for which, as promised above, is as follows.

A necessary God must have necessary contents, necessarily. Since everything about God is necessary, and the world is part of God, then the world must be necessary too. For the Greeks, the necessary thing must be a unity, by definition, but as we can see, Spinoza's proposal would render God complex. Simplicity can no longer be preserved. Thus whatever else is deemed necessary must be internal to this necessary thing, that is, contained within it. There cannot be two necessary beings, for according to this reasoning only God is a necessary being. But that leads to another problem, namely the realization that nothing remains contingent.

This means nothing can be other than it is, resulting in the total denial of freedom. And if everything is settled from the outset, then the passage of time becomes illusory. Time is unreal in a predetermined world.

Hence the attributes that are fragile in the classical scheme are secure here. Omniscience includes the future since advance planning gives knowledge about what is planned. Immutability can be retained for nothing ever changes in a foreordained universe. As with the German railway system (a personal comment on my own Teutonic heritage), everything occurs on schedule. And impassibility can be preserved as there is nothing to get excited or passionate about in a cosmos that is entirely laid out. All three of these attributes can be salvaged, though everything comes at a price. Just look at what we need to give up in order to retain them: not only do we forfeit God's simplicity as well as the temporal process, but we are also required to relinquish free will for both God and humans. Some would claim that this cost is too high. Is this more of a loss or a gain?

Anticipating a discussion that is soon to follow, and still referring to our chart, process panentheism accepts the pantheistic posture that the world is completely internal to God, indicating that the deity is complex, but rejects both the notion that the temporal process carries no meaning for either God or the world, as well as the idea that freedom is precluded for both. In process terms, both God and the world are necessary—the essence of God is to be embodied with a world—yet it need not have been this world with these details. The world that constitutes the body of God could have been different. This world with its particulars is an accident—a non-essential aspect of God. And both retain some freedom of movement (Hartshorne & Reese, 189-97).

It's About Time

Whereas Spinoza added to the otherwise classical picture of divinity the notion that the world is internal to God, here another figure adds instead the idea that God is, at least in part, temporal, meaning in time. This personage is Socinus—an uncle and nephew team, with Laelius as the former (1525-62) and Faustus the latter (1539-1604). Fausto, as he was also called, and his immediate followers gave birth to the Socinian movement.

This group quarrelled with the Augustinian view that sees God as having the privileged perspective on the world from the standpoint of an eternal present, where all of eternity is fully laid out for God in one "now" (although it is difficult to conceive how any sense can be made of this concept of nowness from within this vantage point, for what exactly would "now" mean in this context?). For the Socinians, the passage of time must mean something to God, in fact something similar to what it means to us. A temporal God must have an aspect which is both related to and subject to time. If this is the case, then to be in time entails being subject to change, for everything in our experience changes in reference to time. Nothing is immune from it, and this must apply to God as well. Specifically, as the future slips into the present, it must carry with it new information. This information then imparts new knowledge to both God and ourselves. The future is not there to be known. It must become what it is not, namely the present or past, for it to deliver the goods—for it to convey its contents. Thus God's knowledge must grow. A changing world requires a changing knowledge of it. Every time we point to it, it is different than it was before.

As can be imagined, this idea of a temporal deity did not sit well with the religious authorities. (I seem to recall Jesus as having a similar nemesis.) Hence the teaching of the Socinians earned for them the status of heretics. Since change implies corruptibility, God necessarily undergoes no change. To admit that God is temporal would be judged a defect, unbefitting of a divinity. After all, only matter is subject to alteration and the deity is non-material. Case closed. The way to prevent change is to insist on omniscience as including the future. Yet with this allowance, neither God nor humans can entertain free will in a determined universe, and we are back to the disadvantages of Spinoza. However, if we are unwilling to commit to this, then Socinus offers us a way through the difficulty. God is not omniscient with respect to the future, nor is God immutable or impassible in the classical sense. But on the plus side, free will can now be retained for both humanity and deity. This renders the future indeterminate. Still too odious for some, no doubt, though not if one dispenses with the psychological attachment to the Greek notion of a perfect being (Hartshorne & Reese, 225-27).

The Whole Package

The process panentheistic strategy appreciates the contributions from both Spinoza and Socinus and seeks to combine them. For process thinkers, it makes scientific sense to view God in both terms. If something, or an aspect of it, is in time (as per Socinus), it, or that aspect of it, must also be in space (as per Spinoza), and vice-versa. This is an insight drawn from Albert Einstein's special theory of relativity and is germane to the process outlook. Since everything is now internal to God, that means that everything contained in time and space, including the world, is part of God's spatiotemporality. Very much opposed to the Greek dualistic notion that whatever the world is like, God is unlike, here God and the world enjoy a commonality.

And the two do not fail to interact. The mind of God is the location of God's purposes and will, the contents of which include the values which God hopes the world will aspire to. God's mind then communicates these to God's body—the world. God knows what is best for the world at any given moment and relates this as a type of value set to the world. The world is then free, to the extent that it is able, to act on God's plea. If it heeds the call, then the amount of value in the world increases and this is what God inherits—a world with heightened value. Nor does this procedure have a termination point, but will continue indefinitely, world without end. And in the eyes of proponents of process thought, this now overcomes the dualism of the Greeks, for what the world is like, God is like as well. As the world goes, so too does God, although with certain restrictions. God, for instance, can only ever increase in value, never decrease; so God's kind of change is always in the form of growth and development, not degeneration. The system can never run down, since God is its initiator and propagator.

The reason that there are entities in the world is because God gives each one an address—a place to begin to develop (a set of spacetime coordinates) as well as a reason to marshall its efforts around—an ideal for it to aim toward and grasp. Should the entity find that God's will conforms to its own, then this ideal is taken on and produces a genuinely novel expression (or instantiation) of creativity, one that both God and creatures can enjoy. So God keeps the ball rolling, but there is neither ball nor rolling without God's input. On the one hand, an entity never fails to go without God's influence, and on the other, free will is preserved for both the world and God. Thus God cannot be the lone cause for any event, for that would override the free will of others— something of which the process God is incapable. Panentheists believe that the foregoing makes for a complete picture of divinity, thereby rendering all previous approaches deficient in some way.

But there are consequences. The greater the self-determining power—the process term for freedom—that an entity wields, the more it can forge its own path, whether for or against God's ideal for it. And by the same token, the more creatures that there are with this same amount of power, the more that intentions will clash. Not all production of creativity can be harmonious. We live in a messy world, full of conflict. A far cry from the diagnosis that antagonism results from a fall and a curse. What is more, should the entity elect to go its own way, deciding that God's will does not sufficiently match its own and opting instead for an alternate path, an element of distortion is introduced into the proceedings. In opposition to an increase in value, the world now needs to deal with an increase in evil.

There is a definite advantage to this, however—one that Whitehead himself appreciated. Having experienced the tragedy of losing his son in World War I, the result of his agonizing over this loss left him with the inability to hold to the classical rendition of divinity—where God's omniscience includes the future, thereby leaving no room for free will. Whitehead could not live with a God like this, so he created his own philosophical-theological system in which omniscience is confined to the past and present, and where freedom remains intact. Otherwise it could be argued that if the future, which cannot be altered but at the same time is known from eternity, included the loss of his son, then that must entail that God's plan from the outset contained the item involving his son's untimely death. This would lead to the pernicious conclusion that the death of his son was God's will. For Whitehead, God must fit another description. The problem of evil, or the theodicy problem, motivated him to cast God in a different light. The process solution divests God of all responsibility for evil, since humans become its perpetrators. We are the main ones left with the requisite degree of consciousness and power to generate it. Only we can introduce it and only we can eradicate it, God of course acting as prompter for the latter. Hence there is no guarantee that evil will ever be removed, yet if we want to do something about it, we are going to have to do it ourselves. This leaves God entirely good, though not all-powerful, and us a little bit powerful and potentially either good or evil.

As per Figure 4, with the world internal to God, the deity becomes complex, for God is now made up of parts. The part of God that is the world is now necessary, though not its particulars. The details within the world continue to undergo alteration, but the world as such is an essential feature of the divine. I mentioned that the mind or mentality of God is the eternal essence of God, but that also applies to the fact of the world. The world itself is as eternal as God is, though not what it contains. The process God is never without a world, but the latter never ceases to change the items within it. In comparing ourselves to God, we can conclude that we are different from the divine both in degree as well as in kind. In reference to the temporal aspect of God that is the world, God is very much greater since God contains the entire length and breadth of it. We may be just a drop in the ocean, but we are nevertheless an integral part of it. In terms of the eternal aspect of God, however, the differences form another category. The ocean is large but finite, so the difference between us and it is one of degree. Yet when it comes to eternity, we are comparing the finite with the infinite. These are differences in kind. Thus God is much more than simply the world writ large. Only God boasts an infinite, eternal essence.

How then do the classical metaphysical attributes fare with process modifications? As can be imagined, many are left unprotected. Let's look at five of them. Immutability is now discarded since the temporal aspect of God changes, better yet increases, interminably. As the world changes, so too does God. God develops or evolves (though not in the Darwinian/Mendelian sense involving natural selection) along with the world because the two converge. And like its traditional counterpart, the changes do not occur with God's nature, character, will or purposes, but in the shapes which the world continues to assume. The former are located in God's mind and are thus eternal; the latter are found in God's body and are subject to alteration.

This also leaves impassibility exposed to injury. The detriment it experiences is as follows. For process thinkers, God is not passionless toward the world but has emotional investment in it and is moved emotionally toward it. God both knows and is greatly affected by what occurs in the world. Since the world is in God, so are its contents. Part of the specifics of the world includes suffering. These experiences do not go unnoticed in the divine life. Not only is God familiar with the world's suffering but has an intimate knowledge of it. God is neither unfeeling toward the world nor unacquainted with its sorrows. God suffers along with the creatures. It is curious that so much effort in theological history has been devoted to keeping God immune from emotional vicissitudes, as though this were a failing that belongs solely to humans and would thereby be unworthy of God. On the contrary, process thinkers see the impassible divinity as impoverished, for this God cannot share in the world's joys or sorrows. Panentheists are compelled to announce that the classical camp does not even believe its own scriptures, for there is much about the world and its creatures that the God of the Bible continues to delight in (Proverbs 8:31 and many others).

Now we arrive at the three omni's. Taking omnipresence first, this is a divine metaphysical attribute that can largely be recovered, though for reasons different than in the traditional

view. In the process strategy, the universe is populated with entities. Entities are all there is and God has a hand, or perhaps more
precisely, an index finger, in the development of each, pointing
in the direction that it would be best for each to go. Hence God
is everywhere that there is an entity, for these comprise the only
places where one can be in the world. To be somewhere is to be
an entity, and that is exactly where God is, prompting each entity
to integrate God's will into its own. Thus by definition, God is
everywhere present. Beyond these there is no place, only nothing
and nowhere (Hartshorne, 59). And since everything is internal
to God, God has no external environment. The entity that is God
has only an inside and no outside.

On the topic of omniscience, there is much more of a divergence from the traditional doctrine. To the process mindset, there
is agreement that God knows everything that is possible to know;
the departure occurs with how far this "everything" extends. For
panentheists, God knows all data. The trouble is that data come
only from the past (and in God's case also the present, as only God
can know contemporaries). The future, in contrast, is not there to
be known, since it does not supply data. It must slip into the present in order to function as information. Omniscience, therefore,
does not include the future in the process scheme. Moreover, God
enjoys total recall of all that God has experienced (more than can
be affirmed of us as we age) and loses nothing of value once it has
been attained. Evil is of no value, so it is not inherited.

There is another reason as to why the future is inaccessible to
both God and humans. God knows the world in its entirety, but the
future is indeterminate. This is because God does not know with
certainty how creatures will employ their self-determining power.
Consequently, God must wait to determine what transpires. Thus
the future is open and unsettled even for God. God would be the
greatest possible prognosticator in the universe, yet that would
still not catapult probability into the ranks of certainty.

The main disagreement with the classical theists occurs over
the doctrine of omnipotence. In their camp, anything less than all
the power for God would be inferior to divinity and would propel
those adherents into the unorthodox, if not outright heretical. Yet

to process thinkers, a God who cannot act unilaterally is the superior position, for this enables creatures to exercise some of their own freedom. So much so that human power can actually trump God's in certain cases, namely when they elect to resist the divine recommendation. For God can *point to* and *prompt* but not *push* or *pull* (please pardon the plethora of "p's"). Verbs appropriate for the occasion would include God as acting by coaxing, drawing, enticing and luring. Instead of compulsion, this God acts by advising, recommending and suggesting in impressive ways. God can leave the type of impression that would have an impact.

The three omni's are not "created equally" in the following sense. God can be omnipresent, but this does not exclude us from being present somewhere. God's ubiquity does not prevent us from having a set of coordinates ourselves. God can also be omniscient, yet this does not preclude our finite knowledge. God can know everything that there is to know and we can still know something. The situation is different, though, with omnipotence. If God has all the power, brace yourselves, then we cannot have any. This is what it means to enjoy a monopoly on power—you get to have all of it without residue. The other two omni's are inclusive; this one is exclusive. To wield one hundred percent of the power means there is nothing left over for anyone else (Hartshorne & Reese, 273-85).

So as not to give the impression that process is the final word, some objections are in order. We will focus on two. The first concerns the presentation of God's ideals to developing entities. Each entity experiences (or feels) these ideals, whereupon it evaluates them against its own ideals and then responds to God's. One might wonder if this is an imposition on God's part. I use the term evaluate, but is it more appropriate to speak of being forced to contend, though not comply, with God's ideals? This may very well be the way that process metaphysics operates, but is free will being violated here? That, after all, is the language of compulsion. Does God then do violence to creatures? God's input is a requirement for there to be an entity which develops, but has the line been crossed from persuasion to coercion, so that the latter is in fact built into the system?

A second point is this. Must all forms of resistance toward or rejection of God's ideals bring about an entrance of evil into the world? Can the entity not opt for a different value set than the one God intended while nevertheless producing a legitimate though different good? Or if there are grades of goodness, could it not be a lesser good? Why must it be all-or-nothing? Jesus called us to go the second mile with those who ask us to go one mile with them. Does this mean that going only one mile with them, even if it is done willingly, is thereby evil and not some form of good? That would seem a touch narrow.

What Else Is Open to Us?

Openness is open to us. There are two main revisions that the openness camp makes to the classical picture, namely that God has temporal moments and is not averse to power sharing. But first some prefatory material. Each of the three models believes at least two things about itself, in ways that some might assess as abjectly delusional. First, each sees itself as the truest biblical portrayal. More so than the other two, each posture understands its own approach toward the scriptures as casting a wider net when it comes to thoroughness. Neither of the others is appraised as taking into account the fullest reading of the text. When viewed from the perspective of each position, fidelity to the entire sweep of the biblical message is judged to be lacking in the opposing camps. It stands to reason, of course, that no tradition would proudly declare of itself that it is deficient scripturally. Rather, each one is the most faithful to the biblical witness. Just ask them.

Second, each regards itself as the middle position, charting a course between two extremes. Seeking diplomatically to avoid the errors of less enlightened stances, each considers that it has found the most appropriate mediating path. This is what all three hold in common. What differs is that which is perceived as the erroneous extremes. Process maintains that it resides as a sort of half-way house for those disgruntled classical types who would otherwise assume that the only alternative to the traditional view is atheism. "Not so fast," the process thinkers might declare, "for that would be hasty. Consider us first before the pendulum swings to the other extreme." Openness then shifts the one extreme from atheism to panentheism itself. In its own eyes, the most salutary position becomes the middle ground between classical theism and process, although this investigation will attempt to determine the extent to which open theism occupies the middle turf, or whether it gravitates toward one or the other extreme. And not to leave out the classical model, it too has a self-perception of mediating between two unacceptable opposites, namely promoting one God against the many gods of polytheism and the no divinity of atheism (although the same could be said for most monotheistic traditions, including openness, process, Judaism and Islam, all tracing as they do their theological lineage back to Abraham).

Now that we have dispensed with the preliminary considerations, we can revert our attention to the aforementioned subject matter. The openness proposal draws much of its inspiration from the thought of Jacobus Arminius (1560-1609), of whom we have already spoken. He is a Dutch figure who objected to the Calvinist climate of his day. In opposition to Reformed doctrine, Arminius envisioned both human freedom and free divine response as equally authentic. This makes the God-world relation genuine; without it the relation would be jeopardized. In essence, Arminius was a classical thinker who sought to correct the emphasis on divine sovereignty by stressing free choice. The future, therefore, becomes open both for God and humans, and this is what is open about the openness model, which also goes under the alias of "free will theism." What Arminius did not anticipate, however, was the implications his view would have on theology as a system. As we have seen, tinkering with one feature or attribute causes a ripple or domino effect on certain others. Making God responsive in turn makes the divine partially dependent on the world, and this adversely affects impassibility (Sanders, 91), immutability, independence and the foreknowledge component of omniscience. Needless to say, this created quite a stir in the Reformed huddle. An openness emphasis, though, has its roots even earlier in theological history. The ideological heritage of Arminianism can be traced as far back as the Roman politician Cicero (106-43 BCE). He spoke of the future as indeterminate—awaiting decisions on the part of God and humans. Both enjoy free will and as such the future is open and unknowable in principle (Sanders, 68).

Cicero and Arminius are taken as forerunners of the openness movement, although both of them, including later advocates John and Charles Wesley, retained the classical attributes too strenuously to warrant a departure from the classical view. Like Philo, Arminius attempted to tack on to the otherwise conventional model of God some combination of providential care, divine responsiveness and human and divine free will. Yet this still places these figures firmly in the classical camp while openness elects to go beyond them. Arminian thinking may be radical to Calvinists, but insufficiently so for openness types (Pinnock 2001, 13). Open theists recognize that a proposed fine tuning of the classical model yields adjustments that are more widespread. Greater than half of the metaphysical attributes are in jeopardy when fiddling with one, resulting either in a system that requires overhaul or membership in a different fraternity.

There are certain capacities that a God who goes by the openness description must surrender. In addition to the four listed in the previous paragraph, if God allows humans to exercise free choice, then omnipotence also needs to be capitulated. If humans have self-determining power, as the process thinkers defend, then God is either not in a position to override it (in the process case) or may opt not to (in the openness strategy). For exponents of the openness scheme, God has voluntarily sidelined complete mastery and control, referred to as divine sovereignty, long enough to afford humans the opportunity to exercise some power of their own. Hence God has willingly relinquished a total hold on power and effectively delegated it to us. We have freedom to the extent that God agrees to a self-limitation on God's own. This viewpoint also has a history which is known as the kenotic tradition. Kenosis is the Greek term for self-emptying. Thomasius of Erlangen in Germany, in the mid-nineteenth century, applied this notion to Jesus. In Christ, Thomasius argued, God set aside the metaphysical attributes so as to function in the flesh. Proponents of the openness view adopt this line of thinking in reference to the non-corporeal God.

Process theologians have the following concern about a God who shares power. If God actually parts company with a portion of it, then God no longer possesses the full amount. Panentheists fear that God, like an automobile manufacturer that recalls a certain model of vehicle when it perceives a problem with safe operations, might wrest this degree of power from human hands if the circumstances warrant it. Should this be the case, then God never really lets go of the power, which might be why openness claims that God is still omnipotent even without all of it. If God maintains all the power that God needs yet can still draw upon the resources that God has allocated to the world, then power continues to be on a leash for humans and has not been separated from God. Such a God was never willing to part with it in the first place. Even this disbursement is held in reserve. ("The Lord giveth and the Lord taketh away.") How then would this be a revision of the doctrine? If God deals with the world in an omnipotent way, then this is no different from the standard usage. If God deals in a non-omnipotent way, then why defend the term? The question remains as to how we would recognize if it is one or the other. And maybe we need to find another term to invest in.

To differentiate the classical and openness proposals, please refer to Figure 2. We mentioned that traditional theism allows for a few points of contact between God and the world. Yet if an aspect of God is temporal, as it is for the openness divinity, which freely acts within time, then the contact is much more extensive. The point of contact between an inverted parabola and a circle or sphere, provided they are external to each other, is just that—a point. The maximum contact between two squares, unless superimposed, would describe a line in a two-dimensional plane; and that between two cubes would maximally be a plane in three spatial dimensions. The latter approach increases the surface area and, consequently, the amount of contact. Both God and the world continue to be external to each other, though a temporal divinity greatly increases the contact.

Hence with free will theism there is a deity involved with the world in a way that reveals that God has an emotional investment in it. This divinity has an agenda, but needing to take real freedom into account, God's plans experience modification as human choices are made. God has a will, though if unrealized may be pressed to go back to the drawing board. The openness God is assertive and imposes this will on occasion, more so than the process God but less so than the classical. This God has a wish list, but hopes can be dashed. God may desire something, but that alone will not bring it about. For the openness divinity, human free will means that God will not always get God's way. This God grants and respects (and delights in) freedom of choice and consents to live with some of the consequences. Other results will meet with the imposition of God's will.

On this very topic an immediate criticism surfaces, in that the openness God does not resolve the problem of evil. As we have noted, the classical God who is in control of and determines everything is responsible for all evil; the process God who is master of very little is responsible, they contend, for none of it, since we become the perpetrators of it; and here in the openness camp, God effects some things and is thus responsible for evil to that same extent. The objection can be raised as to why certain things receive God's direct interventionist attention—the divine nod—and not others. Specifically, although once again I hesitate to use this example despite its making the strongest statement, why did the Holocaust not make the cut? Was this not worthy of God's assistance? Some might be provoked to question God's selection process and even declare that this makes God open to the charge of arbitrariness.

Here is another tack that can be taken on the issue of God's will. Openness cites multiple biblical passages where it seems that God even enters into negotiations with certain characters. In Genesis 18, Abraham deliberates with God (or an angelic messenger sent to carry out God's will) about the fate of Sodom and Gomorrah. Abraham urges God not to destroy the righteous along with the wicked and to spare the towns if a number of righteous people can be found there. God accepts the terms. Despite the towns not meeting the requirements, the divine appears to welcome God's servants being part of the decision-making process.

Another example comes from Exodus 32, where Moses pleads for the people who have turned to idolatry and thereby provoked God's anger. In an attempt to stem God's fury against them, Moses intercedes for them by reminding God of the covenant God made with the patriarchs and by appealing to God's pride. Moses contends that God's reputation among the Egyptians would be tarnished, since they might claim that the God of the Israelites is evil, in seeking to liberate the people from Egypt so as to kill them in the desert. This strategy at least mitigated the severity of God's intentions and spared the lives of most of the people.

It could be argued that in both of these cases God was either the first to blink or was receptive to the idea of being given a reason to change course. Here is my comment. To claim that the divine might just be letting off steam long enough to test God's servants so that they would be spurred into action, which is what God may have desired all along, is problematic on two counts. First, if God is in the habit of venting or ranting, then this sounds like a God who emotes, which does damage to classical impassibility. Second and more significantly, to declare that God does not say what God means is to suggest that God plays coy high school games and is not above manipulation.

Of the notions that could be considered holdovers from the classical model, the following five for openness are the most prominent. The first is omnipotence and I have already submitted my reservations about it. One final note, though, to drive home the difference between inclusive and exclusive categories respectively, God can perform limitless good without thereby becoming diminished in goodness, and God can also exercise power without losing any, yet God cannot transfer power over to creatures without suffering a net loss. Confer power, and lose it to that same extent. Power is the only metaphysical attribute to have this property.

To employ a governmental analogy, subordinates may be given a certain portfolio and be placed in charge of an arm of the administration, but they are still under the authority of the head of state. While in their office, these underlings wield power but can be removed from their positions at the behest of the leader. The ruler delegates genuine power and interferes in the operations of this branch only when it is needful. God might function in a similar way. God gives power over to servants, but they do not thereby cease to be servants. Their power is real, and grievances and disputes go through proper channels. God in the Old Testament set up first judges and then kings to govern the people. Appeals could be made directly to God, yet generally God respected the power they were given and so deferred to the leaders that God put in place when rulings were to be given—not much of a leader if all issues are to be brought before God anyway. All power is delegated, but David's and Solomon's power, for instance, were real and the God of the text let them use it. Sometimes unwisely. This is why God deposes kings on occasion, and this is precisely what process dislikes—the fact that power can be taken away at any time. The restraints on God's power could become unshackled if God so chooses (Pinnock 2000, xi). God remains lord, but persons are given actual power. God does not step in every time there is a problem. There are some, however, who wish that God would rather have done so more often.

This scenario, though, plays right into the hands of the openness group, for they would proclaim, "Aha, you see, this is exactly what we mean. Those who have been placed in charge of something derive their power from another source, and that source sees to it that abuses of power are addressed and steps in to correct them. Hence creatures have some power and the Creator preserves all of it." Well then, perhaps there is another approach to take. Using a similar analogy, it becomes a matter of jurisdiction. There are levels of government, such as federal, state and municipal. One does not interfere in the affairs of the other. Leaders of nations have authority over national matters, but governors have authority over state issues. All states may be united under a central banner, but they retain a certain autonomy as states. It is not that presidents, for example, choose not to involve themselves in state level concerns; they are not authorized to. Maybe this is how

God's system works. We as governors of our jurisdictions have authentic power under a divine president who manages a different though related set of priorities. Governors and presidents are not usually in competition over the same turf. There might be power struggles where issues overlap, but this is not the norm. Thus the divinity described here is different from the openness God outlined above, for the former genuinely parts with power and is not generally in a position to pull rank. For nations where there is a stronger centralized government, this analogy will not hold and will appear more like the openness situation. Interesting how political schemes can reflect possible divine policies. And they say church and state do not mix.

The second item retained from the classical model is creatio ex nihilo (creation out of nothing)—a position not officially ratified until the Fourth Lateran Church Council in 1215 (Griffin, 31). Here God freely creates a world as an external environment. Odd, isn't it?, that a doctrine which is supposed to be so blatantly obvious required twelve centuries for the whole Church to get on board. Whence the lengthy hesitation if not for lack of clarity? In the Greek understanding, matter is devalued since it undergoes change and therefore corruption. So the strategy is to ensure that material reality is not deemed as uncreated, for that would make a low-value reality equal in status to the eternal God. The Persian dualism of Zoroaster—a forerunner to the Greek version—saw a constant battle of opposing spiritual forces—between good and evil, light and darkness, and so forth— with the material realm as wearing one of the black hats, since its deterioration and degeneration was a product of the dark side. Christendom had a penchant for Greek thought but it did not want to align itself with this. It recognized a moral duality between spirit and flesh but not an ontological dualism between roughly equal and opposite spiritual forces (for good would ultimately prevail). Their loyalty to Greek thought extended only so far. Unfortunately, they did not carry out a thorough housecleaning.

The third is perfect being theology, though for a different reason than the classical group. More on this shortly. The fourth is the Trinity; and the fifth is an historic Fall of humans (Pinnock 2001, 39-40). I find it curious that an association whose self-understanding includes one of greatest adherence to biblical teaching would insist strenuously on terms which themselves are not biblical. Perhaps the concepts are, but an argument would be required in each case. There is no manifestly necessary reason to assume them. The first four are not strictly biblical; the fifth, as we saw in Part One, is not scientific. And if they are retained, it would be done on philosophical more so than on biblical or scientific grounds.

In addition to the spectra drawn in Figures 1 and 2, there are others that can be used to describe the postures of the three main models in reference to specific issues. Consider these four. As was intimated before, each model has a position on the degree of control that God places on the world. In the classical approach, at least for the Reformed variety, God determines everything and all of the metaphysical attributes apply to this divinity and its economy. The world enjoys no freedom of movement in a thoroughly classical setting. In the process view, God controls nothing, other than giving each entity a place or address to begin to develop (a spatiotemporal locus or set of coordinates) as well as a reason for them to focus their efforts around (the presentation of God's ideal for that entity in the particular situation in which it finds itself). In the middle somewhere lies the openness strategy where God is master of some things. As we noted, this makes God liable to the charge of arbitrariness for God's selection process concerning which things get to receive God's attention. The process group would contend that whatever these things are, they are too many; and the classical squad would insist that they are too little.

The second and third spectra are related to the first. In terms of where evil originates, the rigid classical advocate must admit that a God who foreordains everything is responsible for all of it. The proponent of process thinking declares that creatures with consciousness and sufficient self-determining power must confess to it. In the openness view, both God and humans are responsible, and if we only knew precisely which things God controls, then we would know exactly where to lay the blame. The next spectrum involves a corresponding theme. The issue here is what becomes more fundamental between God's power and goodness or love? Upon what foundation is God's activity based? For the classical crowd, it is built on God's power, which trumps God's goodness. Power is automatic in a classical world, while an argument needs to be made as to how a classical God can express concern. If God from eternity, as Reformed theologians maintain with their commitment to double predestination, has saved some and banished others to eventual perdition, then God's power predominates over God's grace (Pinnock 2001, 82). For the process membership, God's goodness trumps God's power. This God is infinite in goodness and love, whereas we require convincing that God actually wields power. Openness, somewhere in the middle, has a dilemma. The Trinity is pointed to as the basis for a loving social relationship, yet omnipotence is retained as a theological category. Time will tell as to which result will emerge from the outworking of this tension.

The final spectrum concerns the extent to which God undergoes change. From the classical perspective, the Greek notion that change implies corruptibility is endorsed, meaning that God cannot change, for change of any kind is always for the worse. Besides, perfection cannot be improved upon. From the process point of view, God's change is always for the better, since God increases in richness of experience. From the openness angle, an analogy is warranted. Openness sees a watch as undergoing a change that can be evaluated as neither for the better nor the worse. A precision watch needs to change, for that is of optimum benefit for the owner who wishes continually to know the correct time. The watch must keep in step with the time. Time changes neutrally from moment to moment and so must the watch. Thus openness rejects the Greek view that change is always for the worse and they picture God as changing like the watch and time do, with no attached value judgment (Hasker, 132-33).

Recall that the main distinctive for perfection on the part of the Greeks was immutability. In Matthew's gospel, Jesus in the Sermon on the Mount urges us to be perfect as our heavenly Father is perfect (5:48). In the gospel of Luke, Jesus in the Sermon on the Plain (so was it a level surface or not?) substitutes the word "merciful" for "perfect" (6:36). Is the Jesus of Matthew's text asking us to be immutable?, for that is what perfect means to the Greeks. Or is merciful the more accurate designation? For the Greeks, perfection is metaphysical; for the Jews, it is moral. Christianity appears to have followed the Greek view.

Making Friends and Influencing People

So just how in the middle of the spectrum is the openness rendition of divinity? Is it precisely in the middle or does it shift toward one extreme? The move from classical to openness seems to involve an aspect of God as temporal, along with all which that entails. This God operates in the world and, for that, God must brandish a temporal component (which also implies that God cannot be simple). Process theists would applaud this move but would also claim that it is insufficient. For them, an adequate picture of God must involve the world as internal to God. To the openness mindset, genuine human-divine relationships cannot occur without divine temporality; whereas for process they are guaranteed with world internality. With the latter in place, nothing can go without God's influence, for there is a divine input to all events, such that this activity on God's part "is a natural [aspect] of the world's normal causal sequences" (Griffin, 6, 13). Openness is unwilling to go this far.

What must now be decided is the relative import of temporality versus world internality. Do they carry the same or similar weight? How much should be assigned to each? Some, no doubt, would announce that the latter is much more foreign to the classical God than the former, thereby placing openness closer to classical.

A representative historical figure who would fit the openness description is Socinus, who took temporality seriously (and look where it got him and his followers). Openness has not yet made mention of him as part of their theological heritage. Assuming that his presence has not escaped their notice, then we can only presume that this omission is intentional and purely for marketing purposes. It may be difficult for a fledgling movement to promote itself when its potential adherents realize that there is a heretic in their lineage. Even if the charge is unjustified, the well has effectively been poisoned. It could be arduous to gain a following with the recognition that there is a person with questionable theological pursuits in their background. A suspect pedigree of unaccepted exponents, so it might be appraised by the wider traditional community, would then align openness closer to process, boasting as it does little if any of the forebears that classical does. Openness, on the other hand, is more accommodating to certain aspects of classical model history.

The answer as to the degree to which free will theism occupies a mediating position on the spectrum will depend on the perspective of the person giving it. From the viewpoint of either extreme, the posture in the middle will seem like a mild version of the opposite extreme. Anything removed from one extreme will tend to be judged as complicit with the other. Classical theism criticizes open theism for being too process, and process objects that openness is too classical. With whom then would open theists more likely be able to associate and dialogue, representatives of the classical or process crowd? If it is centrally located, then there ought to be an equal amount of each. Yet practice does not always reflect theory. Openness and process come to the same table and interact, while classical sends its regrets. Openness and classical are not really on speaking terms. To put it more bluntly, openness along with process are vilified by the traditional standpoint and are the subject of its vitriol. The quality of the faith of the openness and process membership has even been doubted. The lack of charity on the part of classical proponents has even made its way into print for all to observe. One openness author highlights some of the more caustic remarks (Pinnock 2001, 16-20).

When searching for a reason as to why some classical types imagine themselves as the only rightful gatekeepers of orthodoxy, for they appear to envision themselves as holding all the theological cards, consider the following. Traditionalists, as conservative in nature, are more apt to build fences and walls than bridges. They feel they have more to protect. And maybe what gives openness and process some commonality, enabling them to dialogue, is the shared experience of having departed from the parent group. Both know what it is like to cast off from secure classical shores. For them, a move away from the traditional view entails a convergence of sorts.

Furthermore, classical theists usually entertain an image of God whereby the divinity can accomplish what humans cannot. Where there are human limitations, there are divine abilities. Humans, for instance, cannot see into the future, thus God must possess foreknowledge. When presented with arguments as to the philosophical difficulties associated with these postures, such rational appeals go unappreciated. Reason is set aside for responses like "Well, maybe your God cannot pull it off, but mine can. My God is bigger and better than yours." Rationality gets trumped by faith. If faith can move mountains, they suspect, then it can also conceive of a super-sized God.

Nor does logical impossibility appear to stand in the way for advocates of classical theology. Aquinas, at least, understood that God could not perform the logically impossible and that this does not become a requirement for or a knock against God's power. Yet not everyone followed Thomas in this. French philosopher and mathematician Rene Descartes (1596-1650) believed that not even logic could place a restriction on God's capabilities. If God is above logic, if inconsistency is not an issue, then perhaps the following would also not be an obstacle. The scriptures reveal that there are things that God cannot do. God can neither lie nor swear by a being greater than Godself (Hebrews 6: 13, 18). Incidentally, the Bible also seems to affirm that the divine can neither sin nor alter the past. (Though on the topic of uttering falsehoods, God seems not to be above sending spirits into false prophets to do God's lying for God [1 Kings 22:20-23].) A supralogical God must be able to overcome these impediments as well. If the divine need not follow the law of non-contradiction, then there is nothing to prevent God from, say, promising covenantal benefits but then withholding them even if the conditions are met. Irrationalists are committed to resting content with this, for in their eyes this is the most superior portrait of God—one who can do anything.

Others, however, are prompted to concede that there are in fact some things that God cannot achieve. The God who bestows logic also lives by it (Nash, 38-47).

Another consideration is that none of the three models exhibits a monolithic stance. Instead, there are a range of positions within each tradition, such that if ellipses (or North American footballs) were to be drawn for each approach around its central region (see Figure 5), then there could be a point of contact between adjacent camps if not an outright overlap. Every movement has its liberal and conservative elements, its left and right wings, and each is wider than its stereotypical images. Hence the right extreme of one might be similar to the left extreme of the one juxtaposed to it. This would make Calvinism the right extreme of the classical strategy (or any deterministic scheme encompassing the theologies of Augustine, Aquinas, Luther, Calvin and Zwingli [Hasker, 141]), and Arminianism the left, maintaining both under the classical umbrella. Openness would then see Arminius as the point of departure for its own stance—as it could reside on openness's right most frontier. A similar case could then be made for the relation of openness to process. Specifically, liberal open theists could find greater commonality with conservative panentheists than could others of each of these two types. Perhaps this is where the ideas of Socinus could be located, since he rejected the Trinity as not being a biblical term, whereas free will theists retain it. And liberal process thinkers would not be panentheists

FIGURE 5
Range of Positions of the Three Models

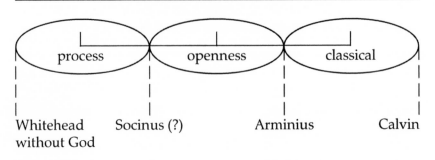

as such, but would hold to the view that Whiteheadian metaphysics is complete in itself and requires no reference to God to make it work. They have been known as "Whitehead-without-God" enthusiasts, where Whitehead's naturalistic theism becomes a full-fledged naturalism.

Do We Have a Prayer?

How do the three models stack up when it comes to prayer? Let's take a well known one—the Our Father or Lord's Prayer (Matthew 6:9-13; Luke 11:2-4)—and determine how each model approaches it. It should be recalled at the outset that the classical view, as we reported, has at least two longstanding camps—the Calvinist/Reformed and Arminian/Wesleyan. Since the former does not really have a prayer, so to speak, given its position on God's sovereignty to the exclusion of human free will, it is theologically, though not practically, committed to the inefficacy of prayer. Their posture makes prayer futile in a world where the future is completely known by God. For this reason, we will concentrate on the latter tradition, where prayer counts for more than, say, praise to God. Their God can also be petitioned to change things.

Our method will be to chart at least the first half of the prayer line by line, allowing all three groups to have their input at each stage.

Our Father—classical—God freely created the world as a contingent, external environment and is thereby its Creator. The language usage of parent, therefore, is appropriate here.

- process—Since God is not the sole cause of anything, God cannot be our creator, so the type of language that conveys the idea that God produced us, as a parent produces its offspring, is unwarranted. God influences rather than produces; God is more a partner than a creator. God is one datum of experience that we take account of and perhaps integrate in our own becoming.

- openness—Creating would be one of the activities about which God enjoys mastery and control. Hence there are grounds for the use of parental language.

who art in heaven—classical—This is where God resides, albeit we are not informed as to whether this is of God's own making or if it is as eternal as God is. Is anything that is external to God also eternal?

- process—Since God has no external environment, there is no place for God to "art." God is the total reality, so heaven could at most be a state of God's mind.

- openness—Same as for the traditional view.

hallowed be your name—classical—God is the height of moral rectitude and thus holy. It is fitting to recognize God as such.

- process—True, though for a related reason. God is infinite love and goodness. It does not get any better than God. God cannot increase in goodness and love, so God is as supremely good as it gets. This is praiseworthy.

- openness—Yes to both.

your kingdom come—classical—Jesus inaugurated the kingdom and God will complete it at the end of the age. History will culminate in the new heavens and earth, where the New Jerusalem will descend from heaven to earth. God will then manifestly be all in all and ruler of all (Revelation 21).

- process—This is much too coercive. God could never unilaterally bring anything like this about, nor could humans contribute to its onset as described in classical terms. A God who operates like this would override human self-determining power.

- openness—This would be another item which God ordains.

your will be done—classical—God holds executive power, which trumps human free will. We thereby acknowledge our rightful place as subordinates. Where God's will and ours conflict, we are to yield to God in submission.

- process—Since God knows the best for us in any given circumstance, it would be most beneficial if we followed the ideals that the wise and just God presents to us. God's will will be done if we accept it, for God can be rejected. In a revised form of the prayer of St. Francis of Assisi, process thinkers would pray that God would "inspire" us to be a channel of God's grace, since we cannot be "made" to comply. And instead of asking God to give us a willing heart, panentheists would pray for God to help us cultivate one. They might also request that God would assist in our becoming open to God's recommendations, for our resolve to be strengthened and our fortitude kindled. This is the extent to which God could act as a parent.

Process thinkers would consider it important to make themselves receptive to the divine will and ask God to inspire or impress upon them the ideals that God intends to present to them. Process prayer makes one open to the values and virtues communicated by the process God.

- openness—Proposing that we determine some things, we might pray similar to Reinhold Niebuhr, circa 1934, that we be given the peace and serenity to accept the things we cannot change (for God has mastery over them), courage to change the things we can (for God has relinquished this amount of power and has delegated it to us), and wisdom to know the difference (for it is not always clear and, besides, not everything should change for the sake of change).

A similar pattern occurs for the remainder of the prayer. A few more comments will suffice. For exponents of process thought, God is certainly concerned about creatures, but a non-coercive divinity is not in a position to extend providential care for them by *giving them daily bread*. God can at best indicate how sustenance might be secured. And again for panentheists, God will *not lead us into temptation*, as God only offers the best ideals for us to grasp and integrate into our own becoming. God may impress upon us where the resistance to God's ideals would lead. Yet God could not *deliver us from evil*, since we are its perpetrators. God could only persuade us to adopt a different course of action. Evil will persist as long as we allow it and make room for it. Yet God can inspire us to become agents of transformation, thereby enabling us to disable the power of evil and arming us so that it can be disarmed. The apostle Paul could have been addressed by the process God when this deity said, "My grace is sufficient for you, for power is made perfect in weakness" (2 Corinthians 12:7-9).

On the basis of these discussions, openness is ostensibly closer to the traditional than the process view. God's not knowing the future does not significantly alter the Lord's prayer for them. Both the openness and process Gods are vision-impaired when it comes to the future, but only process makes the move from God's temporality in the world to the world as in God. The classical group knows no such beast.

Two additional reservations about the process approach will round out our discussion. First, if the presentation of God's ideals for us is automatic, in that God knows which are the best ones and then dispatches them without being asked, then what is left to pray for in the process scheme other than receptivity to those ideals? And if God gives us an appetite for them, what adherents to process thought refer to as a lure for feeling, then need we even request to become receptive to them? It seems that God might already have these things under "control." Second, as intimated before, is the process God a liberal or a conservative? Does God present those ideals which have the greatest likelihood of becoming integrated into developing entities, or stand strictly by the correct aims for the situation, come what may? Does the divinity ever settle for a lesser good or a second best value set, or sternly insist that nothing but the best will do?

Hence prayer for open theists means something. There is efficacy in prayer—it can effect a change. Prayer for a classical Calvinist, however, is pointless if God has already determined the future (and thereby foreknows it). Reformed people still pray and in this way demonstrate another gap between their theory and practice. Prayer for process panentheists amounts to requests for God to instill a change of heart, but this divinity can do little more than affect attitudes. God can neither enforce or enact, yet prayer remains efficacious—for God hears, understands and responds as best God can.

As Clark Pinnock points out, the character of Ebenezer Scrooge in Charles Dickens' *A Christmas Carol* is instructive for prayer purposes (Pinnock 2001, 169). After Scrooge gets through the ghosts of Christmas past and present and is primed or even tenderized to consider seriously the warnings from the ghost of Christmases to come, he is struck by the import of what the future holds. Should events continue on their present course, Scrooge is horrified by the eventual shape they would take. In response, he pleads with the ghost, his appeals are heard and he mends his ways. The future then looks brighter. And this is the thrust of the openness message—with human and divine free will intact (or reinstated) the future is not settled. The content of the vision Scrooge received can yet be altered. Open theists are grateful for Dickens' theological insight. Fiction can serve theological purposes.

Two observations before we close. First, stemming from the above, not only is our being made in the image of the deity a consideration, but the reverse also calls for our attention, for truly do we fashion our gods in our own image. Second, also based on the foregoing, if there is this much uncertainty about the nature of divinity, then, God knows, perhaps it is best not to be dogmatic.

Conclusion

WHERE DO I STAND? A fair question. I am inclined to appraise the process position as going too far, but the openness perspective as not going far enough. I do not have the same confidence in philosophy as does the process approach, nor do I have the same confidence in the scriptures as does the openness viewpoint. I find a tendency for them to overemphasize their allegiance in each case. On this topic of scripture versus philosophy, I would not want to be without either. Each seems to temper the other, and both philosophy and biblical interpretation require continual revision. Having stated this, I am unclear as to how a movement that prides itself on its biblical fidelity (openness) insists on the holdovers that it does from its classical parentage, from which it admittedly departed. Of the items on the list of omnipotence, *creatio ex nihilo,* perfect being theology, the Trinity and an historical Fall, all but one are bereft of scriptural referent. A philosophical supplement does not make them sacred. And since each movement has, and can even be defined by, its extremes (as the saying goes), it is possible to be a fundamentalist regardless of how one describes oneself theologically. Even in a process setting, the writings of Whitehead and Hartshorne can take on an elevated status. Conceptual disputes might then be settled in a similar way as for classical apologists.

At the very least, we can conclude that none of the three areas we have addressed in this study ought to be taken naively, for in each case difficulties ensue. In the first section I indicated my approach, particularly my misgivings, about the Judeo-Christian scriptures and how they are more human in production than

138

perhaps initially supposed. That is, the writings reflect both human gifts, talents, skills and abilities as well as limitations and maybe even foibles. Views of divinity will be likewise affected. In the second part, the world of nature was surveyed in a way that highlights more its supernatural character than commonly held. Consequently, the Bible should not be read literally, since at times alternate interpretations are called for; the world should not be accepted as sensed or perceived, for pure objectivity cannot be achieved and the world and its organisms can surprise us at many a turn; and the Christian God should not be made equivalent to the Greek philosophical God, as neither do the biblical categories always apply to it, nor can the theological system drawn from it stand the strain. On the latter point, some attributes undermine others and cannot strike or broker a peaceful coexistence—they do not mesh together well as a set of doctrines. When one tallies up the conventional attributes, there is only a paradoxical God on the bottom line.

Frustration levels rise and anxiety abounds when there is a lack of clarity, for we cannot rely on the Bible always to say one and only one thing about several important matters. Besides, worship of the Bible is also a form of idolatry ("bibliolatry"). It would be reassuring if we possessed some type of instruction manual when we came from the factory that informed us about what the world is like and what we can expect from it, and that would also direct us so that we would not make avoidable errors or retrace unnecessary steps. Sadly we are left to discover and to fend for ourselves concerning how to function within the world, admittedly with the possible assistance of guardians and educational systems. As thrilling and exciting as this might be, it also comes with potential peril. The theologically conservative among us would be inclined to remind those on the left that God has in fact provided a guide for living in the shape of sacred text. We have noticed, however, that this library of theological reflection did not emerge from a heavenly Xerox machine. It had human help. It is a product, at least in part, of devoted conviction regarding divine activity, and the representation of God it contains might suffer from inaccuracies. The scriptures, it must be confessed, are a useful tool, but even they could stand some refinement. And confidence can be rekindled once it is held that God agonizes alongside us when we do not find our way.

I further wish that there were a third option in addition to God freely generating a world from nothing versus out of something that is already in place and therefore co-eternal with God. The uncreated material that is already there to begin with is the "order out of chaos" view to which some envision Genesis 1:1-2 points, although as mentioned at the outset of our study, this biblical passage could indicate a two-step approach to God's creation. I find both alternatives unsatisfactory. I am also dissatisfied with the classical scheme for the following reasons. As was noted, the program of simply tacking divine care and concern for the world together with responsiveness to it onto an otherwise classical divinity is fraught with problems. What could go wrong? Plenty. Affect one attribute, affect several. Overall, the classical strategy was beneficial initially, but I do not regard it as "permanently binding" (Wheeler, 118). Nor do I recognize the need for commitment to the first formulation of the faith (Pinnock, 184). The most original is not necessarily the best one despite its longevity. What is misguided can also endure.

There is an evolutionary element in all three parts of our study. Scripture develops and adapts to changing circumstances—Jesus was said to have appeared "when the fulness of time had come" (Galatians 4:4)—as does the organized, structured reflection upon it. Nature has evolved in the Darwinian sense and our perspective on it undergoes adjustment as we are introduced to more of it. Some of us see both scripture and nature differently than before. Our views of them have altered and so have they. In the eyes of the Christian world, the Old Testament initiated the New; and organisms adapt to environments which also evolve. This leads to our concept of divinity. Models of deity have evolved to the point where God is claimed to actually experience it. The circle becomes complete. The world and its contents take after the Grand Evolver.

It seems as though power times knowledge equals a constant, for the more knowledge God has, say, about the future, the less power God would possess to alter it. Also, conversely, the more power, the less knowledge (although this is not a knock on body-building). Using the same reasoning, power times love and goodness equals a constant, for the emphasis on one comes at the expense of the other.

On the spectrum of Christian concepts of God, I find myself somewhere in between the openness and process models. Openness holds some promise, but as the youngest of the movements it could stand the most refinements. More so than the others, it is a work in progress. Time will tell if it will. I am also more than willing to accept a temporal aspect to the divinity, as in openness, but I am reticent to affirm that the world is entirely internal to God, as in process. Situated between the two camps, lamentably, does not lend itself to a defensible position of being a little bit world-inclusive. I believe that God is not the total reality and thereby has an external environment. That includes us, and this allows me to enter into relationships with the divine. In my estimation, it is more accurate to think in terms of God as being in the world and continuing to work in history than that the world is in God. I stop short of claiming both that the atom has a psychology and that we are components of divinity.

Yet having committed myself, there are qualities about the planet that have gone unnoticed, or at least underappreciated. Lyall Watson has done yeoman's service in alerting us to the many ways in which the earth and its inhabitants display characteristics usually associated with higher organisms; and these higher organisms sometimes exhibit capacities above those traits ordinarily understood as human. While uncertain that the cosmos is populated with spirits, I do maintain that material reality contains properties beyond what we customarily assume. If neither the world is internal to God, nor if there is a direct connection between material object and spiritual location, as in animistic cultures, the God who created the external environment that is our home appears at the same time to be pleased to use it as a footstool (Isaiah 66:1; Matthew 5:35). Footstools are normally seen as external to those who avail themselves of one. The world is at God's disposal and God is not afraid to use it.

Nor can I envision, despite the schemes of the human heart as exhibiting incessant unabated evil (Genesis 6:5), that the entire length and breadth of a human life is utterly saturated with misdeeds, but can display glimpses or even heights of exemplary activity. Not only in the moral sphere, but also in the artistic world, history records instances of behavior that could actually instill or stoke an amount of pride in the divinity's heart. We are prompted to think upon whatever is noble and excellent (among other virtues)(Philippians 4:8). Acts of bravery, courage and valor could be met with applause from the divine cheering section. The kinds of literary and theatrical skill and craftsmanship that can take our breath away or bring a tear to our eye, and the type of musical virtuosity that can have us dancing in the aisles (unless of course we are attending a symphony) might also initiate the tapping of the divine feet. All three models of divinity are in agreement that God keeps a complete record of all historical events, but does God also play back some of the performances on occasion out of sheer enjoyment, as we would a favorite CD or DVD? All good and perfect gifts may come from God (James 1:17), but God can also receive them. Job might not be the only character in whom the deity takes pride: "Have you considered my servant Job?" (Job 1:8; 2:3) Moses was a murderer, king David was an adulterer and an accomplice to murder, yet David is also referred to as one after God's own heart (1 Samuel 13:14; Acts 13:22). This may not have ended with David. God continues to find things to delight in (2 Samuel 22:20; 1 Kings 10:9; Psalms 35:27; 37:23; 147:11; Proverbs 8:31; 11:20; 12:22; Isaiah 5:7; 42:1; 62:4; 65:18-19; Jeremiah 9:24; Zephaniah 3:17).

One cannot stifle creativity, and God did not exhaust God's supply of it at the end of that sixth mythical day (unless God took a partial shift of duties on the seventh—compare Genesis 2:2 with Exodus 31:17). God is undaunted and continues to interact creatively with the world as an artist who never completely finishes a certain work. And these are not just final or finishing touches but, perhaps, a nurturing activity (such as in a brooding hen metaphor) such that the egg will finally hatch and a new creation will emerge. God only knows the possibilities then!

A Cause for Celebration

IF SOMEONE WERE TO HAVE ASKED the ancient Greek philosopher Aristotle about the cause of a certain event, he would have responded, hopefully not with disdain, "you will need to be more specific." This is because in his estimation there were no less than four causes operative in the world and a complete description or explanation of an occurrence required reference to all four. The standard analogy used to illuminate these four causes comes from construction projects. The materials employed in the building, such as concrete, lumber and nails, are the *material* cause—the substances of which the building is constructed. The muscle needed to erect the structure comes from the laborers, which amounts to the *efficient* cause. The blueprint or plan which guides the workers is the *formal* cause. And finally, the purpose for which those involved go to all the trouble, such as providing shelter from the elements or a place to live or meet or conduct business, is the *final* cause. At the earliest stages of the scientific revolution, Galileo recommended that the emerging scientific method could manage quite nicely by reducing the four causes to two. The latter two did not strictly belong in a scientific description of the world, it was suggested, since they do not lend themselves readily to testing—one of the great hallmarks, distinguishing features or defining characteristics of science—hence they could be de-emphasized. A complete explanation of events no longer required them. Whitehead sought to correct this.

In Whitehead's metaphysical scheme, all four causes are reinstated. Material causes are those subjective becomings which have achieved objective being status and have been relegated to the past as data for future subjects in their next round of becoming. Efficient causes are the influences that these objects in the past project to new subjects in the present. This is how the past impacts or impinges upon the present. The nascent subject is compelled to contend with or take account of these data in its environment, some of which are the products of its previous becomings and having now assumed the status of objects in its own past. Formal causes are the input of information received from God. The divinity presents ideals, out of its store of divine purposes, for each subject to grasp. These ideals are similar to Plato's realm of eternal forms, though whereas for Plato God is a type of super-form, in process thought God contains the forms. Ideals would include beauty and the list of moral attributes outlined for the deity in Part Three. God communicates specific formal causes to each developing entity, whichever value set is best for it in any given situation.

As for final causes, there are two varieties—God's and the other entities. God's input, known as the initial aim, is appraised by the subject for its conformity to the entity's own subjective aim. This means that there are two final causes at work in every event. God hopes that the creatures will take on God's initial aim and integrate and synthesize it into their own development. God's purpose is to maximize value in the universe. The world that entities produce with their self-determining power is the world that God inherits. God wants the best for every creature, in the hopes that this will yield the best product for God to take up into God's own becoming. The creature's purpose is to secure or actualize the vision it has for its own future. If God's will plays into this, novelty is produced and value increased.

What we have just described is how the world works in the process outlook. No explanation of events is complete without reference to all four of these causes. Whereas at Galileo's time, to divide physics from metaphysics meant to separate material and efficient causes from formal and final, Whitehead's world operates with the entire set of four. Both God and the world are therefore both physical and metaphysical. In so doing, Whitehead proposes a strategy to reunite what was cast aside in the early scientific revolution. This is the brilliance of his thought and the genius of his system—that the outworking of his metaphysical scheme has physical implications; the undergoing of his religious process has scientific application. Accepting God's ideals entails a new attitude or mentality, the emergence of the genuinely new that was not there before in that context, and a new shape to the world. Process evolution is through creation as God's ideals are grasped by developing entities; and process creation is through evolution as the world creates a new thing that God inherits. Both God and the world create and evolve.

All four causes reinstated to complete the picture—a cause for celebration.

APPENDIX TWO

A Force to Be
Reckoned With

(The technical material for this piece is drawn from two works by
Ken Croswell and the team of Joel R. Primack and Nancy Ellen
Abrams, both reflected in the bibliographic entries.)

I AM "FORCED" TO "EXPAND" ON THE FOLLOWING. The significance of
this statement will soon become apparent. Whereas the first appendix deals with four causes, here in the second the concern is
with at least four forces.

There are four known forces in the universe, together with a
fifth. First is the electromagnetic force, which accounts for light
and radiation. It also holds the atom together by binding the
negatively-charged electron to the positively-charged nucleus,
containing as it does neutral neutrons and positive protons. James
Clerk Maxwell in 1860 discovered that electricity and magnetism
are related and become united into one force. There are also not
one but two nuclear forces. One is the weak force, responsible for
radioactive decay, among other things. That the earth's interior
is still molten even after roughly four and a half billion years is
due in part to this force. The other is the strong force which binds
quarks—the components of protons and neutrons—into those
composite particles. The fourth force is gravity, keeping us firmly
planted on earth, despite the efforts of high-jumpers and pole-
vaulters (nowhere near the 11.2 kilometers per second or about
40,000 kilometers per hour required for escape velocity).

Gravity is the most prevalent force in the universe and also the weakest. Even where there may be no enduring particles in space and the first three forces are not in play, the effects of gravity might still be felt. In fairness, empty space is not empty, for it contains a temperature, due to what is known as the microwave background radiation (making the universe a type of blackbody). The field of energy therein produces quantum particles that pop into and out of existence in very short order. They do not have enough energy of their own to endure as particles, so they are referred to as virtual. Gravity is the most far-reaching force in that its effects cannot be ruled out even from one end of the universe to the other. The gravitational effects on us from a galaxy at the horizon of what is for us the visible universe is non-negligible. The same cannot be said for the other three forces. In contrast, the strong and weak forces are very short-range, operative only at nuclear scales. All four forces diminish with distance and the weak force has the shortest range. The electromagnetic force would also function at universal scales were it not for a curious feature of the universe, namely that it is electrically neutral. It does not carry a net charge. If it did, the danger is that the repulsive force of like electric charges would overpower the gravitational force and stars would not be able to form by gravity. No stars, no astronomers.

Gravity is bewilderingly weak. The paper on which you are reading these words is acted on by gravity and requires the force of the entire planet to keep it on one's desk. In comparison, we can readily lift it to our eyes and read the message it contains, thereby counteracting all the force that the planet can muster. We can notice the relative strengths of gravity and electromagnetism in a thunderstorm. A lightning bolt can traverse the space between a cloud and the earth's surface very rapidly, yet if an object were to free fall the same distance it would soon reach terminal velocity and require something of the order of minutes to make the trip. Gravity is the only force we need concern ourselves with at universal scales. Conversely, it is the only one we can safely ignore at atomic scales.

There is also a fifth force. Perhaps it is best described in these terms. Albert Einstein drafted the special theory of relativity in

1905 and the general theory in 1915. His personal predilection was such that he envisioned the universe as essentially a stable, unchanging structure on the whole. In order to accomplish this theoretically, he reasoned, in true Newtonian fashion (whose third law states that every action has an equal and opposite reaction), that the attractive force of gravity must be balanced by some repulsive force so as to stabilize the universe. To this end he crafted what he termed the cosmological constant. Later in 1917, his astronomer friend Willem de Sitter pointed out to him that an implication of his general theory was an expanding universe. On the one hand, the universe is a gravitational system, meaning its development can be investigated as an application of the general theory. Edwin Hubble in 1929 detected the redshiftedness of distant nebulae, indicating that distant celestial objects are moving away from us, indeed that most objects are moving away from everything else. It was proposed by Belgian priest and physicist Georges Lemaitre in 1927 that the universe is expanding and affirmed in 1931 that the universe also had a beginning—to be coined the big bang in 1949 by its competitors Fred Hoyle, Thomas Gold and Hermann Bondi who devised the steady-state model of the universe in 1948. The change the universe undergoes can be traced back to an earlier state. On the other hand, the universe has not yet ceased to expand. This expansion might not continue forever, but it has not as yet halted. Einstein abandoned his version of a static universe as well as relinquished his cosmological constant, arguing that it is no longer needed in an already expanding universe.

Einstein was disappointed that he did not believe his own theory. By January 1998 it came to light that he may have been right on both counts. The universe is expanding and it contains a repulsive force. Remarkably, space repels space. To digress for a moment, galaxy clusters are the largest structures in the universe that are bound by gravity. They travel as units. The galaxies they contain might even come in contact at some point. Andromeda, for instance, is the largest galaxy in our cluster, known as the Local Group. Like the Milky Way it is a spiral galaxy though about 60% more massive. The two are on a collision course, the event to occur safely billions of years in the future. Beyond clusters, however, an odd thing happens. The repulsive force dominates and clusters become pulled apart from each other. Note the terminology. Galaxy clusters are not racing through space but are being pulled apart. When space repels space, additional space (what else?) is generated between it. This new space then further repels space. The more space there is, the more of it there is to repel, to the point where new space opens up at an exponential rate. Objects travelling through space are constrained by the limit of the speed of light, but space itself is under no such restriction. This led to the startling realization that not only is the universe expanding but its rate is accelerating. It is expanding ever faster. This now seemingly confirms that it will continue unabated forever. Gravity is insufficient to overcome it.

This repulsion amounts to a fifth force since it is not of the electromagnetic variety. As was noted, the universe does not carry a net charge, so the repulsion is not electric. Instead, it constitutes a force "in the nature of space itself" (Primack, 109).

Having covered the preliminaries, we are now primed to embark on the heart of the "matter." Material reality is subject to the first four forces mentioned. The reason that some matter can be found in the solid state is thanks to the electromagnetic force, which enables chemical reactions to proceed. One of the physical rules that the world must adhere to is known as the Pauli exclusion principle, which states that no two objects can be in the same quantum state. This applies to electrons. If we stub our toe against a chair, we have this principle to blame. When electrons which are bound to the nuclei of the elements in the periodic table come in contact, they cannot be in the same place at the same time. There is no place for them to go, hence they collide. This makes the world, in spots, exhibit hard surfaces.

But what if there were a constituent of material reality that did not interact electromagnetically? The idea is not too far-fetched. There is a notion that spiral galaxies, for instance, contain much more than visible matter, otherwise their energy due to rotational momentum would spew out their contents like mud from spinning wheels. Some of this matter is non-luminous, such as gaseous material between stars that neither shines nor is adequately shined upon. Even though we cannot see it, it can still be detected since it radiates heat. This would not, though, account for all of the mass that is required for these galaxies to remain intact. That is why it has been proposed that the needed matter is non-radiating cold dark matter, undetectable through conventional electromagnetic means. (We can't see it, but these theorists believe that it must be there—sounds a little religious to me.)

Such material would not include the nuclear components we know as protons and neutrons (not protons because they carry electric charge, which makes them interact electromagnetically, and not neutrons since unbounded (free) neutrons readily disintegrate into protons, electrons and antineutrinos), thus the strong nuclear force would also not apply. That leaves gravity and the weak force. Those items that interact weakly are referred to using the unflattering acronym WIMPS (Weakly Interacting Massive Particles). Examples of WIMPS include the elementary particles called neutrinos, which stream forth from the sun as products of nuclear fusion reactions. They are extremely unreactive—they can pass through the earth without even noticing its presence. As a result, they are very difficult to detect, because they hardly ever react with anything—a necessary condition for registering as some type of reading on sensitive equipment. Nor are they very massive, though some believe that they make up part of the required galactic mass to keep them intact, since they are produced in such large quantities. Yet if the galaxy itself is not sufficiently massive, it will be incapable of retaining these particles by gravity.

If certain material does not interact weakly, then all that remains is gravity. Matter that interacts only gravitationally need not be particulate. Joel Primack offers a description of his "double dark theory":

> dark matter move[s] through the ocean of dark energy,... For the same reason that we can't see dark matter, it can't "see" itself; it hardly interacts at all with other dark matter except gravitationally, and thus it can't create much complexity...[T]here is nothing even vaguely reminiscent of the behavior of dark matter. Grav-

ity swings clumps of it around in the presence of other clumps,
but they can pass right through each other. (Primack, 118)

I mention all of the foregoing in order to bring the following into positive relief, and I ask the reader's indulgence in this
highly speculative musing. The issue surrounds how the spiritual
may interact with the material, the transcendent world with the
physical. Some researchers are of the opinion that spirit is an
electromagnetic phenomenon, though we have disclosed certain
difficulties between objects that behave electromagnetically. The
Pauli exclusion principle would compel a spirit to "go bump in the
night" since it would collide with other matter. Or if it be purely
radiation, then it could readily be detected in heat-sensitive equipment, evidence for which is lacking. Nor are they unstable, meaning radioactive, else they would be detectable through the use of
a Geiger counter. That some people understand "cold spots" as
indicative of the presence of spirits and/or their activity suggests
that heat is not the issue, at least not in significant amounts. Hence
a spirit can display none of solidity, light or other radiation. That
they are often reported as white in white dress might prompt us
to declare that they could use a little sun.

Could spirits then be WIMPS? Like WIMPS, spirits are allegedly unreactive, yet unlike WIMPS, spirits are not particulate.
WIMPS may constitute most of the matter in the universe, but
they are cold dark matter. And the matter that they are is particulate and massive, the latter though perhaps not appreciably in
their case. It has been proposed, if fancifully, that upon death a
person loses "21 grams" of weight. (There is also a film of the same
title.) Is this the mass of a spirit? The supposed ability of spirits to
pass through solid objects is also a property of WIMPS. Lastly, if
spirits have mass they could interact purely gravitationally, making them difficult to detect and even making God a type of Great
Attractor, perhaps in the tradition of Pierre Teilhard de Chardin. If
they be energetic, then energy translates into mass (for non-zero
rest mass particles) according to Einstein's special theory of relativity. And if they be massive, then they have a geometry, which
means they generate spacetime curvature and thus exert grav-

ity. If so, then general relativity applies to them as well, for any universe and every dimension has geometry, meaning gravity is present. (Some physicists maintain that the reason gravity appears so weak is that its prevalence throughout all dimensions has caused it to become diluted.) What is more, if, as Primack suspects, the universe is comprised of 25% cold dark matter and 70% dark energy, then could the universe be pervaded by spirits, thereby making the universe very much a spiritual place? 1 Corinthians 15: 35-53 proposes that there will be some continuity between the present physical existence and the spiritual one to come. Perhaps the above reflects that continuity.

One more thing. There are those detractors of process thought who object to its metaphysical scheme. Each round of becoming is characterized by the stages of becoming, being and perishing, only to enhance the next round of becoming by providing for it another being of which a developing entity can make use. Some, like physicist-priest John Polkinghorne, find that this periodic nature or episodic character of the process strategy does not adequately reflect the way the world works (Polkinghorne, 14). Yet an aspect of Polkinghorne's own discipline comes to the rescue. Physics alerts us to a fundamental limitation of spacetime. There are certain measurements of time, length and mass, known as the Planck scale, that require specific minimum amounts. For instance, no object can occupy a space of less than ten to the minus thirty-three centimeters and be greater in mass than ten to the minus five grams else, according to physical theory, it will produce a black hole. One cannot physically squeeze any more material into that space, for then the region would collapse into a black hole. Time also comes with a minimum. The uncertainty principle requires that a change in time multiplied by a change in energy equals Planck's constant. If one lowers the time any further than ten to the minus forty-three seconds, then the increase in energy will also create a black hole. Hence time cannot be measured at scales lower than this amount. A question posed by Robert Mann is "does time exist if there is no clock that can measure it?" Also, "is time continuous or does it come in pieces?" (And in the classic debate between Albert Einstein and Niels Bohr, the issue became whether existence was dependent on measurement. Bohr would have replied in the affirmative; Einstein not.)

One interpretation of time, therefore, is its discontinuity—a type of quantum approach to time where it comes in discrete units or packets. If becoming is quantum-like, that is, if there is discontinuous becoming, then this is consistent with process thought where reality is already episodic. Thus contrary to Polkinghorne's misgivings, process metaphysics evidently has a friend in physics.

(Note: The reference to Robert Mann is from a public lecture delivered by him at McMaster University in Hamilton, Ontario, Canada on October 24, 2008.)

Bibliography

Baigent, Michael. 2006. *The Jesus papers: Exposing the greatest cover-up in history.* New York: HarperSanFrancisco.

Baigent, Michael, Richard Leigh, and Henry Lincoln. 1983. *Holy blood, holy grail.* New York: Dell.

Brown, Dan. 2003. *The Da Vinci code: A novel.* New York: Double-day.

Cobb, John B., Jr., and Clark H. Pinnock, eds. 2000. *Searching for an adequate God: A dialogue between process and free will theists.* Grand Rapids, MI: Eerdmans.

Croswell, Ken. 2001. *The universe at midnight: Observations illuminating the cosmos.* Toronto: The Free Press.

Griffin, David Ray. 2000. "Process theology and the Christian good news: A response to classical free will theism." Chapter 1 in Cobb & Pinnock, eds.

Hartshorne, Charles. 1984. *Omnipotence and other theological mistakes.* Albany: SUNY Press.

———, and William L. Reese, eds. 1963 (c.1953). *Philosophers speak of God.* Chicago: Phoenix Books/U. of Chicago Press.

Hasker, William. 1994. "A philosophical perspective." Chapter 4 in Pinnock, et al.

Holy Bible: New international version. 1978. Grand Rapids, MI: Zondervan.

Holy Bible: New revised standard version. 1989. Nashville: Thomas Nelson Publishers.

Margulis, Lynn, and Dorion Sagan. 2002. *Acquiring genomes: A theory of the origins of species.* New York: Basic Books/Perseus Books.

About the Author

HERB GRUNING, PH.D., has taught a variety of courses in Religious Studies at a number of universities in both Canada and the United States, including McMaster University in Hamilton, Ontario, Canada. He currently teaches at Canisius College, a Jesuit institution in Buffalo, New York. His courses include Religion and Science, and Christian Concepts of God. His main area of research is the thought of the philosopher-physicists Alfred North Whitehead and David Bohm

Dr. Gruning completed his Ph.D. from McGill University in Montreal, Quebec, Canada, in the area of Philosophy of Religion. He graduated from the program with honors (cum laude), and his dissertation was published by the University Press of America under the title, *How in the World Does God Act?* (2000). Blue Dolphin published his second book, *God & the New Metaphysics*, in 2005.

Born in Toronto, Ontario, Canada, Dr. Gruning, and his wife Alice, now live near Niagara Falls, Ontario, Canada.

LaVergne, TN USA
16 September 2009
158116LV00011B/152/P